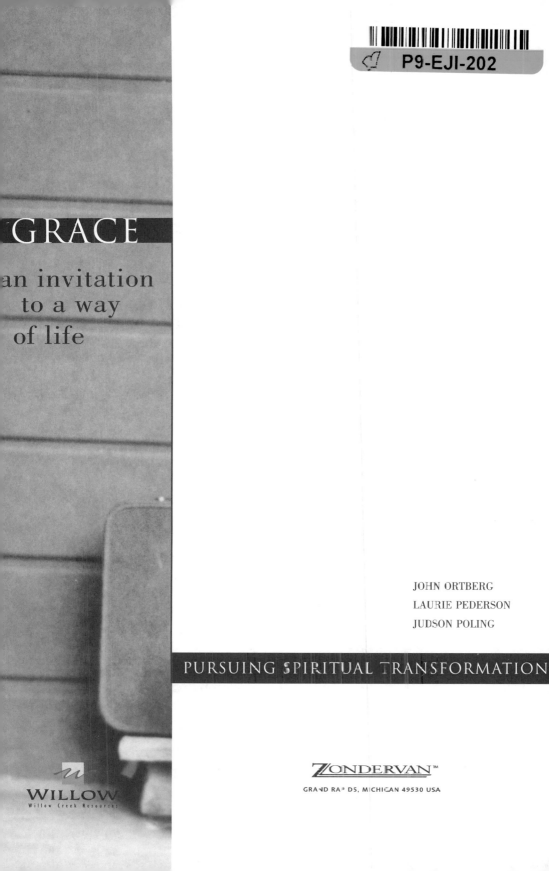

GRACE

an invitation to a way of life

JOHN ORTBERG
LAURIE PEDERSON
JUDSON POLING

PURSUING SPIRITUAL TRANSFORMATION

ZONDERVAN™

GRAND RAPIDS, MICHIGAN 49530 USA

WILLOW
Willow Creek Resources

ZONDERVAN™

Grace: An Invitation to a Way of Life
Copyright © 2000 by the Willow Creek Association

Requests for information should be addressed to:

Zondervan, *Grand Rapids, Michigan 49530*

ISBN 0-310-22074-2

We are grateful for permission given by a number of gifted teachers to use excerpts from their books and messages for the opening readings in the sessions. These authors and speakers are acknowledged throughout this guide.

Interior design by Laura Klynstra Blost

Printed in the United States of America

05 06 07 08 09 10 11 12 /❖ EP/ 24 23 22 21 20 19

CONTENTS

Pursuing Spiritual Transformation

The Pursuing Spiritual Transformation series is all about being spiritual. But that may not mean what you think!

Do you consider yourself a spiritual person? What does that mean? Does spiritual growth seem like an impossible amount of work? Do you have a clear picture of the kind of life you'd live if you were to be more spiritual?

Each guide in the Pursuing Spiritual Transformation series is dedicated to one thing—helping you pursue authentic spiritual transformation. Here, the focus is learning to live in grace. You may discover yourself defining spirituality in new ways. In fact, that's our earnest desire.

You may find this study different from others you have done in the past. Each week in preparation for your group meeting, you will be completing a Bible study and experimenting with a variety of spiritual exercises. These elements are designed to enhance your private times with God and, in turn, to help you invite him into all aspects of your life, even the everyday routines. After all, spiritual life is just *life*—the one you live moment by moment.

It is very important that you complete this work before going to each meeting because the discussion is based on what you've learned from the study and what you've observed as a result of the spiritual exercise. The Bible study and exercises are not meant to be done an hour before the meeting, quickly filling in the blanks. Instead, we suggest you thoughtfully and prayerfully complete them over the course of several days as part of your regular devotional time with God.

A good modern Bible translation, such as the New International Version, the New American Standard Bible, or the New Revised Standard Version, will give you the most help in your study. You might also consider keeping a Bible dictionary handy to look up unfamiliar words, names, or places. Write your responses in the spaces provided in the study guide or use your personal journal if you need more space. This will help you participate more fully in the discussion, and will also help you personalize what you are learning.

When your group meets, be willing to join in the discussion. The leader of the group will not be lecturing but will encourage people to discuss what they have learned from the study and exercise. Plan to share what God has taught you. Try to be sensitive to the other members of the group. Listen attentively when they speak, and be affirming whenever you can. This will encourage more hesitant members of the group to participate. Be careful not to dominate the discussion. By all means participate, but allow others to have equal time. If you are a group leader or a participant who wants further insights, you will find additional comments in the Leader's Guide at the back of the study.

We believe that your ongoing journey through this material will place you on an exciting path of spiritual adventure. Through your individual study time and group discussions, we trust you will enter into a fresh concept of spiritual life that will delight the heart of God . . . and your heart too!

Ten Core Values
for Spiritual Formation

Spiritual transformation . . .

> . . . is essential, not optional, for Christ-followers.

> . . . is a process, not an event.

> . . . is God's work, but requires my participation.

> . . . involves those practices, experiences, and relationships that help me live intimately with Christ and walk as if he were in my place.

> . . . is not a compartmentalized pursuit. God is not interested in my spiritual life; he's interested in my *life*—all of it.

> . . . can happen in every moment. It is not restricted to certain times or practices.

> . . . is not individualistic, but takes place in community and finds expression in serving others.

> . . . is not impeded by a person's background, temperament, life situation, or season of life. It is available right now to all who desire it.

> . . . and the means of pursuing it, will vary from one individual to another. Fully devoted followers are handcrafted, not mass-produced.

> . . . is ultimately gauged by an increased capacity to love God and people. Superficial or external checklists cannot measure it.

Grace: An Invitation to a Way of Life

T he LORD is my shepherd . . ."

It is a phrase that has inspired countless works of art, but it is not meant to be merely a picture. It is beautiful to speak, but it is not meant to be poetry. People read it at funerals, yet it isn't about death. Instead, it is *an invitation to a way of life*. It is the confident statement that it is possible to live in the unceasing care of a relentlessly attentive and gracious God.

Can you make this confident statement? Does it describe *your* way of life? Or do you live worried and weighted, dulled to the daily presence of the Shepherd? You know you were saved by grace, but what does it mean to *live* by grace?

Jesus was the first person on earth to understand and continuously live the Twenty-third Psalm. His Father was his Shepherd every moment of every day.

Jesus moved about in the midst of relentless demands and difficulties, but he allowed himself to be led to green pastures and quiet waters. He lived with a regularly "restored soul." He had no place to call home and yet was content—*joyfully* content. He did not *want*. Living moment by moment in his Shepherd's presence was enough.

In the ordinariness of sparrows and lilies, loaves and fish—and in the extravagance of costly perfume—he had eyes to see a steady flow of his Shepherd's gracious gifts. His cup ran over and he drank in every drop. It's no wonder that at dinner parties and seaside gatherings, at a wedding feast and a well encounter, he made everyone else's cup run over, too.

Even on the cross, in the valley of death itself, Jesus held on to the promises of his Shepherd. Even when he couldn't see or feel the Father, he committed his spirit to him. Jesus persevered in that path of righteousness for his Shepherd's name's sake. And for *your* sake, too—so you could live in the Shepherd's gracious presence forever.

"The LORD is my shepherd . . ."

What would *your* days look like if this was really true for you? How would your life be different—your anxieties, joys, confidence, obedience, freedom, fruitfulness—if you truly lived in the every-day grace of the Good Shepherd?

We invite you to find out.

SESSION
ONE

Living in Grace

The LORD is my shepherd, I shall not be in want. He makes me lie down in green pastures, he leads me beside quiet waters, he restores my soul.

—PSALM 23:1—3A

Reading by John Ortberg

How many "ordinary" examples of God's grace do we experience every day and fail to even notice?

L iving in grace requires new eyes. We must learn to see God's everyday grace at work all around us.

Jesus was the master of this. For him, it was simply apparent that we live in a God-bathed world. He saw that we are surrounded by evidences of God's gracious shepherding. "Look at the birds of the air; they do not sow or reap or store away in barns, and yet your heavenly Father feeds them. Are you not much more valuable than they?" (Matt. 6:26).

Some time ago, my wife and I were watching two geese and their goslings eat. One adult and nine little goslings were devouring the grass, while the other adult stood watch. "Look at that mother goose watch over her family," Nancy said.

"How do you know it's the mother?" I asked. "Maybe it's the father goose."

"No, it's always the mother who sacrifices herself for the family. It's the same in every species."

Just then, the two adults traded off. The eater started watching and the watcher started eating. I was so grateful.

Jesus said that anytime you see a bird nibble some seeds, you are watching the grace of God at work. It's such an ordinary event that most of the time we fail to even notice it. But it is not a random accident that food is available. It is the Good Shepherd at work. Every time you wake up, think a thought, or enjoy a meal, these are not random occurrences; they are gracious gifts from the hand of the Good Shepherd.

How many "ordinary" examples of God's grace do we experience every day and fail to even notice? In the rush of our days, in the preoccupation of our agendas, how many provisions of the Shepherd do we race past altogether?

The Discipline of Noticing

The practice of noticing is a skill.

If we want to live in grace, we must develop eyes that *see*. We must learn what might be called the discipline of *noticing*.

To notice something—to truly pay attention—is a powerful thing. Children demand it. Spouses feel hurt without it. If you have ever been so caught up in watching a basketball game on TV or reading a great book that you didn't notice how much time had passed, you've known what it is to pay deep attention to something. You became *absorbed* in it.

The practice of noticing is a skill. It involves learning to pay attention to gifts that we otherwise take for granted. Stop for a moment and try it. The breath you just took, the way your eyes are reading these words, the working of your mind to understand and learn—*notice them*. They are not accidents. Nor are they entitlements. They are gracious gifts. And what's even more amazing is that their Giver is lovingly present with you even as you are experiencing them.

The sight of a garden blooming in a riot of color, a cold glass of water on a hot afternoon, an encouraging word from a coworker, a warm blanket on a chilly night, the taste of your favorite food, a long conversation with a good friend. All ordinary, but all grace nonetheless. Train yourself to notice, to pay attention, to become absorbed in the grace of your Shepherd.

Seizing Ordinary Moments

Just as we must learn to see Jesus' ordinary gifts of grace, we must learn to seize his ordinary *moments* of grace—moments that the Shepherd would like to use to replenish and refuel us.

A lunchtime walk, a moment of solitude in the car or on the train, the still of the house when the baby is napping, sitting with a glass of iced tea in the backyard. Each can be transformed into a personal and private time of "green pastures and still waters"—*if* you have eyes to see and the willpower to slow down. Your Shepherd has provided everything necessary to transform your rushed soul into a restored one. But he won't force you to turn aside. He won't tackle you to get you to lie down. The choice is yours.

Your Shepherd has provided everything necessary to transform your rushed soul into a restored one.

I Shall Not Want

When our spiritual eyes begin to work, we become aware of his grace all through our days. Our lives become filled with genuine gratitude instead of with ceaseless discontentment. "The LORD is my shepherd, I shall not be in want"—I lack *nothing*, the psalmist says.

Phillip Keller, a twentieth-century shepherd, writes about his experiences on his sheep ranch. He describes one sheep who had the fatal flaw of discontentment:

> She was one of the most attractive sheep that ever belonged to me. Her body was beautifully proportioned. She had a strong constitution and an excellent coat of wool.... But in spite of all these attractive attributes she had one pronounced fault. She was restless—discontented—a fence crawler....
>
> No matter what field or pasture the sheep were in, she would search all along the fences ... looking for a

loophole she could crawl through and start to feed on
the other side. It was not that she lacked pasturage.
My fields were my joy and delight. . . . It was an
ingrained habit. She was simply never contented with
things as they were. Often when she had forced her
way through some such spot in a fence . . . she would
end up feeding on bare, brown, burned-up pasturage
of a most inferior sort. . . .

. . . She was a sheep, who in spite of all that I had
done to give her the very best care—still wanted
something else. She was not like the one who said,
"The Lord is my Shepherd—I shall not want."

—*A Shepherd Looks at Psalm 23*

To say "I shall not be in want" doesn't mean we have
no significant requests or needs. It certainly does not
mean we should be passive in the face of injustice or
poverty. Not wanting means being *settled*. Settled that
the Shepherd knows our real needs. Settled that his pastures really are more lush than the burned-up ones we
habitually pursue. Settled that he can be trusted to provide the best gifts.

In his grace, he does so all the time.

Not wanting means
being settled. *Settled*
that the Shepherd
knows our real needs.

SPIRITUAL EXERCISE

The LORD is my shepherd, I shall not be in want. He makes me lie down in green pastures, he leads me beside quiet waters, he restores my soul.

—Psalm 23:1—3a

Read these words each day this week. Let them sink in. Consider writing them out, paraphrasing them, or committing them to memory. Your challenge is to *live* with those words today. Specifically, experiment with the following:

Today I Will Notice

I will try to have eyes that see God's gracious daily provisions, even in the ordinary—a warm bed, a closet full of clothes, a comfortable pair of shoes, a hot shower, the ability to see, hear, walk, think, feel.

I will look for examples of God's grace around me—in scenes of natural beauty, in the face of a friend, in wholesome pleasures that bring me joy, in my church body gathered in worship.

Today I Will Give God the Opportunity to Restore My Soul

I will be open to ways, large or small, that God wants to lead me to green pastures or quiet waters, and I will consciously try to be with my Shepherd there.

As you go through the week (and throughout this whole study), consider keeping a journal of your experiences with this exercise. How were you stretched to do life differently? Did you find yourself becoming more aware of God's ordinary acts of grace in your life? How were you nurtured and restored? What effects did you notice on your level of contentment? What aspects came easily? What was frustrating?

NOTE: Whatever impression you might have from your reading of Psalm 23, David's life was anything but smooth and serene.

After killing Goliath, David's rise to prominence enraged the insecure and arguably insane King Saul. David was literally stalked by Saul. Forced to live as a fugitive, David narrowly escaped multiple assassination attempts.

David was also no stranger to crushing grief. Jonathan, his most trusted friend—one who "became one in spirit with David" (1 Sam. 18:1)—was killed along with Saul in battle. David also lost an infant son and a grown son to death.

David knew shame and regret. He not only committed adultery, he engaged in an elaborate cover-up scheme. When that didn't work, in desperation, he caused the offended husband to be killed. Confronted by Nathan the prophet, David finally repented, although it was a horrible stain on his public and private reputation.

David also had daily pressures from his role as political and military leader of the nation. His kingdom was threatened by civil war and he was forced to run for his life. His pain was multiplied because his very own son, Absalom, led the rebellion.

The unvarnished emotions accompanying life's ups and downs flow through David's many psalms:

I am worn out from groaning; all night long I flood my bed with weeping. ...

—Psalm 6:6

Be merciful to me, O LORD, for I am in distress. . . .My strength fails because of my afffliction, and my bones grow weak.

—Psalm 31:9–10

> *Answer me with your sure salvation. Rescue me from the mire, do not let me sink; deliver me from those who hate me, from the deep waters.*
>
> —Psalm 69:13–14
>
> Against this landscape—one punctuated by pressure, opposition, fear, grief, guilt, uncertainty—David confidently asserts, *"The LORD is my shepherd."* As you meditate on the Twenty-third Psalm during the coming weeks, keep in mind the turmoil of David's life circumstances. Whatever you discover about the Good Shepherd of David's soul, realize that God acted this way on behalf of a man embroiled in personal and national uncertainties. None of these problems could prevail against the powerful grace God offered.

1. As you read through the first three verses of Psalm 23, imagine for a moment that none of it is true. Paraphrase the psalm below so that it says just the opposite ("The LORD is *not* my shepherd—God does *not* care for me"). What would your life be like if those statements were reality?

2. Some people view God as distant and uninvolved with his people—like an absentee landlord—yet in Psalm 23, God is compared to a loving shepherd. Use the following chart to contrast a landlord with a shepherd.

Characteristic	Absentee Landlord	Shepherd
Dwelling place		
Frequency of contact		
Emotional involvement		
Personal, individual knowledge of tenants/sheep		
Expected involvement when danger appears		
Relative dependency of tenants/sheep		

In light of these contrasts, summarize what God being *your* Shepherd means to you.

3. Read John 10:7–18 and 27–30. What does Jesus call himself in verses 7–9?

What does he mean by this figure of speech?

What does he call himself in verse 11?

What additional facts do we learn about this Good Shepherd in verses 11–15 and 27–30?

4. As strange as it may seem, it is not always easy to get sheep to lie down. They tend to resist rest, for instance, when they are fearful (sheep are easily panicked) or competing with others (sheep are prone to turf wars). What kinds of things make *you* resist lying down in the Shepherd's care?

5. The sound of flowing water might sound refreshing to us, but it is frightening to sheep. A shepherd must find still waters or the sheep will not drink. Describe a "quiet waters" experience you have had recently. What part does God play in bringing about such an experience? What is our responsibility?

6. The phrase "He restores my soul" connotes bringing something back, a returning or regrouping. Isaiah 49:5 uses the same verb to mean *gather* and Isaiah 58:12 translates it as *rebuild* in the sense of restoring destroyed streets and houses. Psalm 19:7 says the law of God *revives* the soul, using this same verb. With that as a backdrop, what concrete ways do you think David needed this gracious work in his life? How about you?

7. Knowing God as your Shepherd leads steadfastly to contentment. That contentment doesn't come from always getting your desires; it comes from trusting that what God gives you is *enough*. Consider these words:

What if God says no? What if the request is delayed or even denied? . . . If God says, "I've given you my grace, and that is enough," will you be content? Content. That's the word. A state of heart in which you would be at peace if God gave you nothing more than he already has.

— Max Lucado, *In the Grip of Grace*

Rate your overall life "Contentment Quotient" right now according to the following scale:

1	2	3	4	5
very content	somewhat content	not feeling much of anything	mildly discontent	regularly discontent

How can you be authentic with God about your desires while still cultivating a contented spirit?

8. What are the greatest barriers in your life that keep you from seeing God as a green-pasture-loving, still-water-giving, soul-restoring Shepherd?

My summary of the main point of this session, and how it impacts me personally:

> NOTE: You will fill in this information after your group discussion. Leave it blank until the conclusion of your meeting.
>
> In the next session the spiritual exercise *follows* the Bible study and requires setting aside a block of time to engage in personal review and confession. Please look ahead to that study and do some advanced planning to allow enough time for yourself to complete the spiritual exercise.

SESSION
TWO

Grace for Regrets

*He guides me in paths of righteousness for his
name's sake.*

—PSALM 23 3B

Reading adapted from a message by John Ortberg

*Then one day came
the Fall. There
appeared on the
mauve sofa a stain. A
red stain. A red jelly
stain.*

S ome years ago, we traded in my old Volkswagen
SuperBeetle for our first piece of new furniture: a
mauve sofa. From the moment the sofa arrived, we
had clarity on rule number one in the house: *Don't sit on
the mauve sofa.* Don't eat on the mauve sofa. Don't breathe
on, look at, or think about the mauve sofa. Remember the
forbidden tree in the Garden of Eden? "On every other
chair in the house you may freely sit, but upon this sofa,
the mauve sofa, you may not sit, for in the day you sit
thereupon, you shall surely die."

Then one day came the Fall. There appeared on the
mauve sofa a stain. A red stain. A red jelly stain.

My wife, who loved the mauve sofa, assembled our
three children in front of it. "Do you see that, children?
That's a stain. And it's not coming out. Not forever. And
that's how long we're going to stand here until one of you
tells me who put the stain on the mauve sofa."

There was silence for the longest time. No one said a
word. I knew they wouldn't, for they had never seen their
mother so upset. I knew they wouldn't because they knew
that they would spend eternity in the "time-out chair." I
knew they wouldn't because I was, in fact, the one who

had put the stain on the mauve sofa, and I knew I wasn't saying anything.

The Stain of Sin

The truth about us is, of course, that we've all stained the sofa. Some stains are small, barely noticeable. But some of them bleed through the entire fabric of our lives. These are the stains we regret in the cold, small hours of the middle of the night, wishing we could relive some moment and get it right this time. We genuinely struggle with the reality of living in grace.

Because of this, God has given us the practice of confession. It is important to say that confession is not about prying mercy from God's fingers like prying an Oreo from a child's hand. It is about our being healed and changed. When we bring our sins out of darkness back to God's light, two things happen. First, we are liberated from guilt and refreshed in the reality of grace. Second, we are a little less likely to sin in the same way in the future. God's paths of righteousness will begin to look and feel more attractive.

Confession is not about prying mercy from God's fingers like prying an Oreo from a child's hand. It is about our being healed and changed.

How do we practice confession in a way that begins to heal and transform our souls? Let's think about it as a six-step process for spiritual stain removal.

Preparation

I begin by placing myself in the care of the Spirit and asking for help. Apart from this, confession is dangerous. If left to myself, I am prone to mauling myself for things I ought not to feel guilty about or glossing over truly ugly stains that demand attention. Confession always starts by placing myself under the protection of God, asking for *his* light to shine in the right place with the right intensity.

Self-Examination

I must take some time to reflect on the thoughts, words, and deeds of my life, acknowledging that I have sinned. I open myself to God's gaze. As Richard Foster states in his book *Prayer*, "Far from being dreadful, this is a scrutiny of love. . . . Without apology and without defense we ask to see what is truly in us. . . . It is for our good, for our healing, for our happiness."

Confession should be specific and concrete. One admission of "I lied to my boss and said I was working when I wasn't because I wanted to avoid trouble" can bring about more change than twenty episodes of "I haven't been truthful enough."

Confession also involves taking appropriate responsibility for what I've done. I hate doing this. What starts as a confession often ends up an excuse: "I didn't mean to yell at you, but I had a bad day." To confess means to own up to the fact that my behavior wasn't just the result of bad parenting, daily circumstances, or a chemical imbalance. Those things may have been involved, but somewhere in the mix was a *choice,* and the choice was made by me. It doesn't need to be excused; it needs to be forgiven.

Frequently I sin while attempting to meet a legitimate need in an illegitimate way.

Perception

I need to see my sin with new eyes, new insight, new understanding. Along these lines, one question can be very helpful: "When did I depart from the 'path of righteousness' and *why?*"

I may find that I lied in order to escape painful consequences that would have resulted if I had been honest. Or I may discover that I gossiped about someone because I was feeling jealous or insignificant.

This is critical because often sin is tied to some need or another. In fact, frequently I sin while attempting to meet a legitimate need in an illegitimate way. If I don't address those needs in proper ways, I'll go right on sinning.

Maybe I need to learn to experience the love of God more fully so I can be liberated from petty jealousy that makes gossiping almost irresistible. Or maybe I need to tolerate a higher level of pain in my life for the sake of speaking truth, when lying could get me out of a tight spot.

A New Feeling

True confession is not just an exchange of information; it involves entering into the pain of the one I've hurt and into God's pain over sin. The apostle Paul called this "godly sorrow" (2 Cor. 7:10). This fitting emotional response to my wrongdoing leads me to genuinely say, "I'm sorry," and to seek reconciliation; it pushes me to change and grow. It is hopeful pain, leading me to grace, not to sustained shame.

It is important to look at your own tendencies in this regard. You may be among those who live under an inordinate amount of guilt and who feel responsible for everything. A minor slip and you feel like Jack the Ripper. You will have to lean extra-hard into grace. For others, it's just the opposite. You blame others even when it *is* your fault. If that is you, you will have to push yourself to be ruthlessly honest about your sin.

A New Resolve

In addition to naming what I've already done, confession involves my intentions about the future. As God does his work in me, I feel a deep desire not to do this hurtful thing again. I resolve that, with God's help and the help of others in Christian community, I will change. This may very well involve setting right what I did wrong.

This was the determination of Zacchaeus: "Here and now I give half of my possessions to the poor, and if I have cheated anybody out of anything, I will pay back four times the amount" (Luke 19:8).

It is the level of resolve that helps me know if I'm actually repenting—literally "turning away" from my sin—or just attempting damage control. Of course, I can give no guarantee. But genuine confession involves a sincere intention at least.

The Summit: Healing Grace

The final step in confession, the top of the mountain, is grace. Not just grace as an idea, but the reality of it,

> *It is the level of resolve that helps me know if I'm actually repenting—literally "turning away" from my sin—or just attempting damage control.*

being immersed in it, given life by it. God-honoring confession should begin in sorrow and end in joy.

In the movie *The Mission*, Robert de Niro plays a thoroughly cruel, selfish, brutal man. As an act of penance, he is required to carry with him a heavy burden tied to his body. It weighs him down. It causes him pain. But through carrying the burden, he begins to see his life differently. All he had built his life around has, in reality, been a burden to him and hurtful to others. He begins to see his own helplessness.

One day, on a desperate climb up a mountain, it becomes apparent that he is not going to make it. He couldn't carry the burden. It would kill him. Then a man standing nearby, with one stroke of his knife, cuts it off and de Niro is free. The burden has done its work.

The giving of the burden was an act of grace. It caused pain and hardship, but it was grace all the same. The release from the burden was also an act of grace.

So it is with confession. Through it we feel the weight and pain of our burden. And through it we come face to face with the One who, with a stroke of his knife, sets us free.

1. Another one of David's most famous psalms is Psalm 32. In it, David talks about a difficult time in his life when he was not living in integrity. Read through the psalm, and notice that after he sinned, David did something we can all relate to (found in the first few words of verse 3). What was that?

   How does the truth of Proverbs 16:25 relate to this human tendency?

   Why do you think we tend to do that when we sin? Get specific—when was a recent time you did that and why did you do it?

2. Verses 3 and 4 of Psalm 32 describe "life in the foolish lane"—where integrity is lost, and secrets are kept. Put into your own words what that experience must have been like for David.

3. What did David finally do to end this episode in his life (Ps. 32:5)? What did God do?

4. Psalm 32:8–11 is like an amplification of Psalm 23:3 (where God guides us "in paths of righteousness for his name's sake"). What style of leadership does God *not* want to exercise (Ps. 32:9)?

What comparisons can you make between our attitudes toward God's leadership and the unwillingness of animals to come under the control of their owners? If God is so great and loving and concerned for our well-being, why do we *ever* resist his direction?

5. Read Psalm 51, another great psalm of forgiveness. When we sin, our human tendencies cause us to either try really hard to do something to earn forgiveness, or to grovel in despair, convinced our condition is hopeless. According to verse 1, what is true about God that makes both of these responses unnecessary (and ineffective)?

6. What additional light does 1 John 1:9 shed on our responsibility and God's responsibility in the matter of forgiveness?

NOTE: A distinction must be made between three kinds of forgiveness: forgiveness available, forgiveness applied, and forgiveness enjoyed.

God makes forgiveness *available* to all humans, but it is not applied or enjoyed by those who haven't trusted Christ for that forgiveness. Forgiveness is *applied* to all true Christians the instant they receive grace through the merits of Christ. Forgiveness *enjoyed* comes only after we accept what we already have, and feel it in our experience.

Consider this analogy: A rich aunt sets aside $100 million for you (it's available, though not yours yet). Upon her death and the reading of the will, that money gets transferred to your account (now it's applied). Yet you will live like a pauper until you access the money (and enjoy it).

Likewise, when we confess our sins individually and experience God's forgiveness, we are simply "making withdrawals" from the gracious resources of our heavenly Father. He's already transferred into our account a complete pardon. Verses like 1 John 1:9 teach us how to enjoy forgiveness in our experience. If we are Christ-followers, "the blood of Jesus, his Son, purifies us from all sin" (1 John 1:7) as a once-for-all act of grace.

Confession of individual sins is not some sort of mechanical process—put in the quarter, out comes forgiveness; rather, we live under the umbrella of a secure relationship with God. Our adoption by God isn't threatened by any of our failures.

We need to enjoy and feel free in the forgiveness that's ours. As Paul wrote, "only let us live up to what we have already attained" (Phil. 3:16).

As a Christian, available forgiveness is already applied forgiveness in your case. The only thing that remains is for you to enjoy that gift through staying in close relational connection with Jesus. Confession doesn't obtain for you anything new; it makes real in experience what's been yours since the day you came to Christ.

7. When God leads us in "paths of righteousness," it reflects *his* character and it benefits us. That's why David says it is ultimately "for his name's sake." Psalm 106:6–8 and Ezekiel 36:22–32 speak of two episodes in God's dealing with Israel echoing this same supreme motivation. With these passages as a backdrop, explain how God's forgiveness of you reflects who he is.

How can this truth enrich your walk with God?

SPIRITUAL EXERCISE

S et aside a block of time this week (we suggest an hour or two) to engage in personal review and confession. Allow the outline below to guide your time. If helpful, use your journal to record your thoughts and feelings as you go along.

Preparation

Place yourself under the guidance, protection, and care of God, asking for *his* light to shine in the right places with the right intensity. Perhaps pray the following prayer or one like it:

> *Precious Savior, why do I fear your scrutiny? Yours is an examen of love. Still, I am afraid . . . afraid of what may surface. Even so, I invite you to search me to the depths so that I may know myself—and you—in fuller measure.*
>
> —Richard Foster, *Prayer*

Self-Examination—*When Did I Sin?*

Prayerfully reflect on your thoughts, feelings, and actions during the past week. Remember, confession will be growth-producing and grace-giving only if you let down your defenses.

Be candid and concrete. What were some specific points of departure—moments when you clearly left God's paths of righteousness, choices you made that do not reflect life as Jesus would live it? (Note: Sometimes, we deviate from the path to pursue an activity that is wrong; other times, we sidestep an activity that is right. Both kinds of sins—commission and omission—take our feet off the road God wants us to walk.)

Perception—*Why Did I Sin?*

Ask God to give you fresh insight and understanding regarding your sin.

Are there any patterns of which you need to take note? Are you able to discern the *why* of your departure from God's path? What is the legitimate need behind your choice? How can you rightly meet that need?

A New Feeling—*What Were the Results of My Sin?*

Can you feel the hurt of those you offended—including God? Allow yourself to experience appropriate, godly sorrow.

A New Resolve—*What Are My Intentions Now?*

Resolve that, with God's help and the help of others in Christian community, you will embrace growth and pursue change. Commit to doing whatever may be necessary to make it right.

Experiencing Healing Grace

Allow your forgiving, grace-filled Shepherd to "cut the burden from your back." Picture the load of sin, the weight of guilt, the cords of shame falling from you into a deep cavern. Hear it crash far below you and then feel the earth shake as a landslide covers it up forever. By the grace of God, feel yourself stand up straight, tall, and free!

Close your time by reading David's Psalm 103.

TAKE-AWAY

My summary of the main point of this session, and how it impacts me personally:

NOTE: You will fill in this information after your group discussion. Leave it blank until the conclusion of your meeting.

SESSION THREE

Sustaining Grace

Even though I walk through the valley of the shadow of death, I will fear no evil, for you are with me; your rod and your staff, they comfort me.

—PSALM 23:4

Reading adapted from a message by Bill Hybels

Rather than looking to God for direction and help, Asa panicked.

I t happened early one summer morning in a Burger King restaurant. I was in a melancholy mood because of a particular pressure in my life that was weighing me down and showing no signs of relief. I had gotten to that point where my human strength to endure was nearly gone. I happened to be reading the story of King Asa in the Old Testament.

Asa was a pretty good king overall. He led a moral life; he exercised fair and kind leadership; he had removed false idols from the land; he generally honored God in everything he did. God's favor and blessing was being poured out on his life and his leadership.

Then one day, a neighboring nation gave indication that it was going to attack Asa and God's people. Rather than looking to God for direction and help, Asa panicked. He ran out and made a treaty with one of the most godless, corrupt kings in the area. He thought he was being smart. The potential invaders would certainly back off when they learned of this multinational treaty. Little did he realize what forming that treaty did to the heart of God.

To God, that alliance was betrayal. It was like a swift kick in the stomach. In effect, it was Asa saying, "Well, God, I knew you couldn't be trusted with this problem. I knew you didn't care enough to come alongside. So I went to Saddam Hussein for help. You know, someone I can *really* trust."

"When problems get hard enough, when pressures get high enough, don't bet the farm on God." That's what Asa's actions really communicated.

As I was reading this story, I was anxious to find out how God was going to respond to Asa's turning away. How do you think God responded? He sent a prophet to Asa telling him that if he had bet the farm on God, God would have certainly come through for him. He would have handed the invading nation over to Asa's hand, no problem. "But now," the prophet says, "you have done a foolish thing."

"When problems get hard enough, when pressures get high enough, don't bet the farm on God." That's what Asa's actions really communicated.

"Since your heart is no longer completely the Lord's, since you no longer trust him fully, since you have decided he's not worth betting the farm on, God has released you from his protection plan. You are officially on your own now," the prophet, in essence, said. If you read the rest of Asa's life story, it's not very pretty. He made a tragic mistake when he bailed out on God.

The prophet's parting words were these:

For the eyes of the LORD move to and fro throughout the earth that He may strongly support those whose heart is completely His.

—2 Chronicles 16:9 NASB

Review these words carefully. Picture them. God's eyes are moving to and fro. He's restlessly searching the earth for someone—*anyone*—whose heart will trust him completely. And when he finds such a person, he's going to strongly support that man or that woman. He's going to come alongside. He's going to help. He's going to be present and powerful no matter how big the problem or how high the pressure.

Betting the Farm on God

There I am, in the Burger King. It's still dark outside and I have a backbreaking weight crushing the inner life out of me. My mind is already spinning about "Plan Bs"—thinking about alliances, thinking about dark, stupid, foolish things.

Have you ever been there? Have you ever come to the absolute end of your human endurance? Maybe it was physical pain, or maybe it was emotional upheaval that had your foundations rocking. Maybe it was a family breakdown with a spouse or a child that threatened to shatter your fragile heart. Do you remember when you were there?

Perhaps you are there right now and you feel panicky. You wonder what you are going to do to survive. You are starting to doubt that God can be trusted with your problem.

No treaties, no compromises, no Plan Bs. I will not take matters into my own hands. I will look to you alone.

In my moment of deep distress, after just having read about Asa, I decided I needed to do business with God right then. I wrote out 2 Chronicles 15:9 in my journal and started praying it through to God. I said, "God, I see you just as this verse describes. I see you searching the planet—your eyes going to and fro—searching the globe looking to strongly support someone with a backbreaking problem. I've got that kind of problem. You say that your only qualifier is that I demonstrate a willingness to trust you completely. Well, here I am and here's my heart. I'm going to bet the farm on you in this deal. I'm going to abandon every other pain-reducing plan that has been spinning around in my head. No treaties, no compromises, no Plan Bs. I will not take matters into my own hands. I will look to *you alone*."

As mystical as it sounds, I felt a strange kind of relief come over my heart. In Philippians 4:7, the apostle Paul calls it "the peace ... which transcends all understanding."

It is difficult to describe, but unmistakable when it happens in your heart.

The peace came, in part, from realizing that I was not a victim any more. I was not trapped. I left the restaurant with a renewed sense of hope—that God would strongly support me through this. That I would make it. The problem didn't go away that moment, or that day, or the next day. But I decided to wait on him, to stay fully committed to him, to trust him to bring either a solution or the strength to keep the problem from debilitating me.

I would have to say that hidden moment in the predawn hours in the Burger King was the richest moment of that summer. God's presence and grace were so real to me. The peace was sweet and pervasive. Do you know what you are going to find true about Christianity? Your richest, deepest, most precious moments are not going to happen in crowds of people. They will be the hidden ones when you're at the end of your endurance, when you are walking through your own dark valley and you make one of those trusting covenants with God.

The peace came, in part, from realizing that I was not a victim any more. I was not trapped.

Do you know what God is doing right this moment in human history? Among other things, he is restlessly scanning the planet looking for someone whose back is breaking because of a pressure or disappointment or a grief or a worry or tiredness or temptation.

Are you in desperate need of some strong support? Then he is saying to you, "I will meet you in the middle of whatever it is. I will come to you with power and gentleness. I will strongly support you in this. I will either provide a solution or I will give you my grace to bear up under it and walk out on the other side. The deal is, though, I need you to bet the farm on me."

All he's looking for is a *yes*.

BIBLE STUDY
AND SPIRITUAL EXERCISE

This Bible study and exercise is designed to help you walk through a current "dark valley" situation of your own, bringing God's promises powerfully to bear. We suggest that you set aside a block of time to complete this reflective experience. Find a time and place free from distractions. As you begin, welcome God into your thought life. Be completely candid with him. Invite him to speak strongly to you as you bring your burden to him.

1. The emphasis for your thoughts is verse 4 of Psalm 23:

   Even though I walk through the valley of the shadow of death,
   I will fear no evil, for you are with me; your rod and your staff,
   they comfort me.

   Take a moment to paraphrase this verse in your own words.

NOTE: What is the "valley of the shadow of death"? In the original Hebrew, the words translated "shadow of death" are all actually just one word. This term does not necessarily just mean the time immediately preceding death (as it is often understood). The literal translation is "deep darkness." Job 24:17 uses the term to describe the darkness that people try to hide in when they cover evil actions (see the context in Job 24:13–16 and 34:22). Psalm 107:10–14 similarly uses the term to describe the feeling that accompanies rebellion against God, and Jeremiah 13:16 says deep darkness can be God's judgment. It can describe confusion (Job 12:22), sadness (Job 16:16), or physical places like a lonely desert (Jer. 2:6) or a mine shaft (Job 28:3). It can signify the darkest moments of the night (Amos 5:8). It is certainly no coincidence that the prophet Isaiah used this term when he predicted the coming of Jesus, the One who ultimately dispels spiritual darkness (Isa. 9:2). So when you read that God is with us in the valley of the shadow of death, realize it is a rich phrase that encompasses all of life's dark, overwhelming experiences.

2. David talks *about* God in verses 1–3 of Psalm 23, but in verse 4 he starts talking *to* God. What observations can you make about this change and the subject matter of the fourth verse?

NOTE: In his book *A Shepherd Looks at Psalm 23*, Phillip Keller observes, "During this time [the summer, when sheep have been led out to the mountain ranges] the flock is entirely alone with the shepherd. They are in intimate contact with him and under his most personal attention day and night. That is why these last verses are couched in such intimate first-person language."

3. Turn your attention to what has been troubling you lately. Where do you find your mind drifting to when you're not doing something? Is there a situation about which you can't seem to stop worrying? Identify that specific concern below:

4. Now go one step deeper. How do you feel about the situation? Why does it seem so overwhelming?

Pinpoint your greatest fear about this matter:

God, if you don't come to my aid . . .

5. Is there any way you're considering a "Plan B"? Tell God honestly about any compromising or sinful options that look good to you, or to which you are afraid you are going to fall prey. Maybe you've dabbled or even gone headlong into such a plan. Specifically identify any such actions (or intentions) right now:

6. What are you hoping God will do? What is the answer to your problem? If you don't know what to ask for, tell God that:

God, please . . .

7. Is there anything you sense God's telling you to do? Are there any aspects of the problem that could be improved by your choice or actions?

8. Verse 4 of Psalm 23 speaks of *walking through* dark valleys in life. What is the significance of the motion David describes— what is the truth about valleys, their duration, and our spiritual progress?

9. Psalm 23:4 also says to "fear no evil." Note that it does *not* say there will be no evil in our lives. In your own words, expand on what this verse promises.

10. There were several uses for a shepherd's rod, which was a short, clublike instrument. Ezekiel 20:37, Leviticus 27:32, and Jeremiah 33:12–13 describe one of those uses. What is it?

NOTE: In addition, a shepherd would use his rod to examine the wool of his sheep, parting it and looking for skin sores or parasites. The rod was a weapon which could be thrown at a predator or used as a club (see 1 Sam. 17:34–35, where such use is implied). And a shepherd might also throw his rod near a wayward sheep or one approaching poisonous weeds to warn it.

In light of how a shepherd used his rod, how might God's rod be a source of protection to you?

11. A shepherd might use his staff to rescue a sheep tangled in a thicket or stuck in mud. Shepherds would also nudge their sheep with the staff, indicating the direction to walk. Sometimes just the touch of the crook was enough to reassure a sheep—it was a way for a shepherd and sheep to "stay in touch." How might God's staff show up in your current situation and be a comfort to you?

12. Read 2 Chronicles 16:9. Apply the first half of verse 9 to the "deep darkness" problem you identified earlier. Put in your own words what God offers you in this situation.

13. Read the following two passages. Summarize God's promises, specifically as they apply to your situation

    Isaiah 40:28–31

    Isaiah 43:1–3

14. You've heard God's promises and commitment to you. Now it's your turn to declare your intentions and "bet the farm" on God. Write your own expression of trust to him.

    Finally, this week, take David's words with you—"Even though I walk through the valley of the shadow of death, I will fear no evil." Whenever you feel trust eroding and fear welling up, dwell on those words. Remind yourself in that moment that *you* are cared for by a gracious and powerful Shepherd.

TAKE-AWAY

My summary of the main point of this session, and how it impacts me personally:

> NOTE: You will fill in this information after your group discussion. Leave it blank until the conclusion of your meeting.

SESSION
FOUR

Delighting in Grace

*You prepare a table before me in the presence
of my enemies. You anoint my head with oil;
my cup overflows.*

—Psalm 23:5

Reading adapted from a message by John Ortberg

*What keeps me
from joy is often a
preoccupation with
myself and my own
little agenda.*

S ome time ago, I was giving a bath to our kids. Johnny was still in the tub, Laura was out and safely in her Carter's, and I was trying to get Mallory dried off. She was in no particular hurry. In fact, she was doing what has come to be known in our family as the Dee Dah Day dance. This consists of Mallory running around and around in circles, singing over and over again: "dee dah day, dee dah day."

It is the dance of great joy. When words are inadequate and she is too happy to hold it in any longer, she has to dance to release her joy. But on this particular occasion I was irritated. "Mallory, hurry!" So she did. She began running in circles faster and faster and chanting "dee dah day" more rapidly.

"No, Mallory, that's not what I mean. Stop with the 'dee dah day' stuff and get over here so I can dry you off. Hurry!"

Then she asked a profound question. "Why?"

I had no answer. I had nowhere to go, nothing pressing to do. I was just so addicted to hurry, trapped in the rut of moving from one task to another. Here was life, here was joy, here was an invitation to the dance right in front of me, and I was missing it.

Ironically, what keeps me from joy is often a preoccupation with myself and my own little agenda. That very selfishness keeps me from noticing and delighting in the myriad of small gifts God offers each day.

But for Mallory, life is not that way. She just lives. While she's taking a bath, it's a dee dah day moment. When it's time to get dried, that's another one. After she's dry, it'll be time for another. Life is a series of dee dah day moments. Not every moment is happy, of course. There are still times that call for tears. But each moment is pregnant with possibility. She doesn't miss many of them. She is teaching me about joy. And I need to learn.

Joy Is God's Destiny for You

"God is the happiest Being in the universe."

Joy is at the heart of God's plan for human beings. Joy is at the heart of grace. And the reason is worth pondering: joy is at the heart of God himself. My guess is that most of us seriously underestimate God's capacity for joy. He also knows sorrow. But the sorrow of God, like the anger of God, is his temporary response to a fallen world. It will be banished forever from his heart the day the world is set right. Joy is his basic character. In the words of Dallas Willard, "God is the happiest Being in the universe."

As creatures made in his image, we are to reflect God's fierce joy in life. The Bible speaks not just about our need for joy in general, but for that particular kind of joy which characterizes God. After teaching on the need for obedience, Jesus told his friends, "I have told you this so that *my* joy may be in you and that your joy may be complete" (John 15:11). The problem with people, according to Jesus, is not that we are too happy for God's taste; it is that we are not happy enough.

The apostle Paul put it like this: "Rejoice in the Lord always. I will say it again: Rejoice!" (Phil. 4:4). This is a command. Joylessness is a serious sin—one to which religious people are particularly prone, and perhaps the one most tolerated by the church. How often have people misunderstood God because they attributed to him the grim, judgmental, defensive, soul-wearying spirit of many who claimed to be his followers?

We have badly underestimated the necessity of joy. The prophet Nehemiah tells his people, " . . . the joy of the LORD is your strength" (Neh. 8:10). Think about those words. Joy is strength. Joy produces energy. Its chronic absence will create weakness. In the words of Dallas Willard, "failure to attain a deeply satisfying life always has the effect of making sinful actions seem good." If we label all joys and pleasures as unspiritual, it can actually *weaken* us in our efforts to live godly lives.

Strategic Celebration

People who want to pursue joy need particularly to practice the discipline of celebration. This is a primary reason why the Old Testament puts great emphasis on feast days. Times of feasting were to be transforming experiences—just as times of meditating or fasting were.

Celebration generally involves the practice of activities that naturally bring us pleasure—gathering with people we love, eating, singing and dancing playing, surrounding ourselves with beauty—and as we're doing these things, reflecting on how gracious God must be to have given us such wonderful gifts.

When we celebrate, we exercise our ability to see and feel goodness in the simplest gifts of God. We are able to delight today in something we wouldn't have even noticed yesterday. Our capacity for joy increases.

Begin Now

The psalmist says, "This is the day the LORD has made; let us rejoice and be glad in it" (Ps. 118:24). What day is he talking about? Two verses earlier, in Psalm 118:22, it says that "the stone the builders rejected has become the capstone." In other words, what everyone else thinks is

The problem with people, according to Jesus, is not that we are too happy for God's taste; it is that we are not happy enough.

worthless is actually used by God as vital and strategic in his building. This time of acceptance by God even in the midst of rejection by people is the very day we are told to rejoice in. Therefore, any day—and every day, each with its shortcomings—is the day we can see God work. It is the day God made, and which Christ's death redeemed. If you are going to know joy, it must be in *this* day.

How much of our lives do we spend waiting to live—waiting to experience joy? We believe the illusion that joy will come someday when conditions change. We go to school and think we'll be happy when we graduate and get married. We get married and decide we'll be happy when we have kids. We have kids and decide we'll be happy when they grow up and move out. When they do, we lament that we were happier when they were home. If you are going to know joy, it must be in this day.

Joy in this world is most always joy in spite of something.

This raises an obvious question. Can joy be genuinely embraced even in the presence of pain, frustration, or suffering? It is here that we make one of the most surprising discoveries about joy—often it is people closest to suffering who have the most powerful joy. People who were close to Mother Teresa say that instead of being overwhelmed by the suffering, she fairly glowed with joy. An officer imprisoned by the Nazis with Dietrich Bonhoeffer (a German pastor who was later executed by Hitler) said about him, "He always spread an atmosphere of happiness and joy over the least incident and profound gratitude for the mere fact that he was alive."

Joy in this world is most always joy in spite of something. It is a "defiant nevertheless." It is a joy that holds tight to the belief that God has not yet written the last chapter—and that when he does, joy will reign unblemished and uninterrupted.

If you don't rejoice today, you will not rejoice at all. If you wait until conditions are perfect, you will wait until you die. *This* is the day that the Lord has made. *This* is the Dee Dah Day.

SPIRITUAL EXERCISE

A dd verse 5 to your daily reflections on Psalm 23:

You prepare a table before me in the presence of my enemies. You anoint my head with oil; my cup overflows.

Your spiritual exercise is to live in joy, as best you can, each day for one full week. Ask yourself this question, "What would *this day* be like if I allowed God to 'prepare a meal' for me, to 'anoint my head with oil,' to 'fill my cup' to overflowing?" Here are a few ideas, but by all means feel free to invent your own ways to enjoy life with your gracious Shepherd.

- When you sit down for a meal, imagine your Shepherd preparing the table just for you. Slow down, enjoy the gift of food in his presence.
- Consider planning a celebratory evening with your small group or family—just to delight in God's goodness together.
- Pursue a favorite activity this week. Try to consciously engage in it with the Lord as your companion.
- Be particularly aware of little joys as you go about each day. Take note of relational moments, moments of scenic beauty, meaningful accomplishments, moments that make you laugh.
- When you worship with the church body this week, express your joy directly to God for the ordinary and extraordinary ways he has made your "cup overflow."
- When irritations and frustrations arise, resolve in your mind that you will choose joy.

If this is a particularly painful era for you, some of these ideas may feel awkward. God doesn't want you to pretend. But resolve, as best you can each day this week, to hold on to "nevertheless joy." Ask the Lord to prepare a table for you even "in the presence of [your] enemies." Consider making a list of all the blessing you have in God, even in the middle of the difficulty.

1. In common language, to "prepare a table" (Ps. 23:5) means to make a meal and then set the table. Shepherds obviously don't prepare a physical table for sheep; but shepherds do prepare high, grassy areas—tablelands or *mesas* (the Spanish word for table)—for their sheep by scouting them out ahead of time, eradicating any poisonous plants, and ensuring the water holes are clear from obstructions. What are some of the ways God prepares a table for us as his sheep in everyday life?

2. The shepherd's hard work for his sheep takes place in the presence of enemies—bears, lions, and cougars all live in the same areas as sheep. What parallels can you make between this fact and the good things that come from God to us in a fallen world?

3. Enjoying God's goodness is so important that we are commanded to do it regardless of circumstances. What insight do you gain from the following verses in this matter of enjoying God's provision even in the presence of enemies?

Philippians 4:4–7

James 1:2–4

Habakkuk 3:17–19

4. Do you think that by asking us to give thanks in everything (1 Thess. 5:18), God expects us to live in a state of denial? Explain your answer.

5. Rate your opinion on a scale of 1 to 5 (1= Strongly Agree, 5= Strongly Disagree) of the following statements:

___ Pursuing pleasure tends to lead to wasted time or even harm.

___ I think a lot more about work than about play.

___ I'm uncomfortable if I think I appear overcome with happiness or joy.

___ Life is hard; now and then I get a little relief.

___ Life is great, though sometimes I need to be more serious.

___ My friends consider me a joyful person.

___ I have less fun now that I'm a Christian.

What do your answers tell you about your personal tendencies toward joy and pleasure?

6. What pleasures do you think are unspiritual? How can you tell? (See Eph. 5:1–10.)

What sins start looking attractive to you when you deny yourself legitimate pleasures?

What light does Colossians 2:20–23 shed on inappropriate denial of pleasures and true godliness?

How might times of laughter and fun free you from a distorted view of yourself or God?

7. As you look back over the recent past, have you become a little soul-weary and joyless? If so, what has contributed to that mood? If not, what has kept your joy factor high?

8. Rejoicing is so important that God commanded special times for celebration. What do you find out about the value of "sanctified partying" from the following passage?

Deuteronomy 16:9–15

9. Rejoicing is so important, it ought to take place in the midst of worship. What do you learn from Psalm 149:1–4 and Psalm 150 about the need for times of all-out celebration as we worship corporately?

10. Ecclesiastes 3 tells us there is a time for various activities and feelings in life, including a time to laugh and dance (v. 4). According to Ecclesiastes 2:24–25, what role does God play in our ability to enjoy the simple pleasures of life?

How does that truth currently apply to your life?

TAKE-AWAY

My summary of the main point of this session, and how it impacts me personally:

NOTE: You will fill in this information after your group discussion. Leave it blank until the conclusion of your meeting.

SESSION
FIVE

A LEGACY OF GRACE

A Legacy of Grace

*Surely goodness and love [mercy] will follow
me all the days of my life.*

—PSALM 23:6A

Reading adapted from *A Shepherd Looks at Psalm
23* by Phillip Keller

*How many of us are
truly convinced that
no matter what
occurs in our lives we
are being followed by
goodness and mercy?*

All that has gone before in the Twenty-third Psalm is
now summed up by the psalmist in one brave but
simple statement: "Surely goodness and mercy shall
follow me all the days of my life!" The sheep with such a
caring, attentive shepherd knows that, no matter what
comes, goodness and mercy will be in the picture.

How many Christians actually feel this way about
Christ? How many of us are truly convinced that no matter what occurs in our lives we are being followed by
goodness and mercy?

Of course, it is very simple to speak this way when
things are going well. If my health is excellent, my income
is flourishing, and my friends are fond of me, it is not
hard to say, "Surely goodness and mercy shall follow me
all the days of my life."

But what about when my body breaks down? What do
I say when I stand by helpless, as I have had to do, and
watch a life partner die by degrees under appalling pain?
What is my reaction when my job folds up or when my
friends prove false and turn against me? When my world
is falling apart and the dream castles of my ambitions are

crumbling, can I honestly declare "surely—yes, surely—goodness and mercy shall follow me all the days of my life"?

In looking back over my own life, I can see again and again a compassion and concern for me in my Master's management of my affairs. There were events which, at the time, seemed like utter calamities; there were paths down which He led me that appeared like blind alleys; there were days He took me through which were as black as night itself. But all in the end turned out for my benefit and my well-being.

With my limited understanding as a finite human being, I could not always comprehend. With my natural tendencies to fear, worry, and ask "why," it was not always simple to assume that He really did know what He was doing with me. There were times I was tempted to panic, to bolt and leave His care. Somehow I had the strange, stupid notion I could survive better on my own.

Do I leave goodness and mercy behind me as a legacy to others, wherever I go?

But despite this perverse behavior, I am so glad He did not give me up. I am so grateful He did follow me in goodness and mercy. This to me is the *supreme* portrait of my Shepherd.

A Legacy of Goodness and Mercy

In ancient literature sheep were referred to as "those of the golden hooves"—simply because they were regarded and esteemed so highly for their beneficial effect on the land.

Sheep eat all sorts of weeds and other undesirable plants which might otherwise invade a field. And, more than any other livestock, they richly and effectively fertilize the soil. In my own experience as a sheep rancher, I have seen two derelict ranches restored to high productivity and usefulness. What previously appeared as depressing eyesores became beautiful, park-like properties of immense worth.

In other words, goodness and mercy had followed my flocks. They left behind them something worthwhile, productive, beneficial to both themselves, others, and me.

Where they had walked there followed fertility and weed-free land. Where they had lived there remained beauty and abundance.

The question now comes to me pointedly, is this true of my life? Do I leave goodness and mercy behind me as a legacy to others, wherever I go?

On one occasion two friends spent a few days in our home while passing through en route to an engagement in the East. They invited me to go along. After several days on the road one of the men missed his hat. He was sure it had been left in our home. He asked me to write my wife to find it and send it on to him.

Her letter of reply was one I shall never forget. "I combed the house from top to bottom and can find no trace of the hat. The only thing those men left behind was a great blessing!"

What do I leave behind? Sometimes it is profitable to ask ourselves such simple questions as:

Do I leave behind peace—or turmoil?

Do I leave behind forgiveness—or bitterness?

Do I leave behind contentment—or conflict?

Do I leave behind joy—or frustration?

Do I leave behind love—or rancor?

Do I see sinners with the compassion of Christ or with the critical eye of judgment?

There remains in my own mind boyhood recollections of the first stories I was told about Jesus Christ as a man amongst us. His life was summed up in the simple, terse but deeply profound statement, "He went about doing good!"

His good and kindly acts were always commingled with mercy. Where so often other human beings were rude and harsh and vindictive of one another, His compassion and tenderness was always apparent. Even the most flagrant sinners found forgiveness with Him, whereas at the hands of their fellow men they knew only condemnation and cruel criticism.

Again, I have to ask myself is this *my* attitude to other people? Do I sit on my pedestal of self-pride and look with contempt upon my contemporaries, or do I get down and identify myself with them in their dilemma and extend a small measure of the goodness and mercy given to me by my Master?

Do I see sinners with the compassion of Christ or with the critical eye of judgment? Am I willing to overlook faults and weaknesses in others and extend forgiveness as God has forgiven me my failings?

The man or woman who knows firsthand about the goodness and mercy of God in his or her own life will be warm and affectionate with goodness and mercy to others. This is to be a benefit to them, but equally important, it is to be a blessing to God. Yes, a blessing to God!

Nothing pleased me more than to see my flock flourish and prosper. It delighted *me* no end to feel compensated for the care I had given them. To see them content was wonderful. To see the land benefiting was beautiful. It was a reward for my efforts and energy. In this experience I received full compensation for all that I had poured into the endeavor. But most of us forget that our Shepherd is looking for some satisfaction as well. This is the benefit I can bring to Him.

He looks on my life in tenderness for He loves me deeply. He sees the long years during which His goodness and mercy have followed me without slackening. He longs to see some measure of that same goodness and mercy not only passed on to others by me but also passed back to Him with joy.

He longs for love—my love.

Then He is satisfied.

> *The man or woman who knows firsthand about the goodness and mercy of God in his or her own life will be warm and affectionate with goodness and mercy to others.*

Taken from *A Shepherd Looks at Psalm 23*. Copyright© 1970 by W. Phillip Keller. Used by permission of Zondervan Publishing House.

PURSUING SPIRITUAL TRANSFORMATION

SPIRITUAL EXERCISE

Your exercise this week is to pause once in the midst of each day (consider establishing a specific time that will be the same each day) and reflect on the following two questions:

Where Is God's Goodness?

How is God's goodness and love following you this day . . .

in mundane moments
in times of warm fellowship with him
in moments of disappointment
when you feel anxiety and fear
even when you have let him down

Where Is My Goodness?

How have you been an agent of goodness and love this day? In what ways are you living "as if the Shepherd were in your place" by extending grace to others, perhaps through . . .

simple acts of kindness
really listening to someone
conveying dignity and respect to people you encounter
a loving touch
a truthful word
extending help to those in need

This is not an act of confession. We need to see what we get right as well as what we get wrong. Focus on how God's grace flows through you. If you feel you've fallen short, simply receive God's gracious offer of a fresh start.

1. Take several minutes to review the eras of your life using the chart that follows (or if you need more space, create your own on a separate sheet of paper). Follow the instructions written below to fill in information step-by-step.

   A. Reflect on each era, specifically identifying some of the low points. Put a label on those events that you remember, and list those "dark valleys" under each era.

   B. Consider God's involvement in those events. Did you feel at all exposed or uncared for? If it was during a time you weren't a believer, how did you wish God would have helped? Even if you were a believer, you may still have longed for God to do more. Note honestly to what extent in the midst of the problem you sensed—or didn't sense—God's goodness and love.

   C. Now consider the outcome of those experiences. In what ways did God's goodness and love pursue you despite those dark times? Even though you may not have felt it at the time, how was he at work behind the scenes? How has God turned those things around for some good in your life?

   D. Move on to consider high points in the various eras of your life. Put a label on those events or seasons.

   E. What was God doing in those times to show his goodness and love? How have those experiences contributed to the person you are today?

	Childhood and Youth	Adulthood
A. Dark valleys		
B. Sensed God?		
C. Good that's come		
D. High points		
E. Good that's come		

NOTE: The Hebrew word for "follow" in Psalm 23:6 literally means "to chase." One way to picture this is to imagine two little puppies nipping playfully at the heels of their master—because God's goodness and love nip at your heels your whole life. Another picture is of a tracker who is able to follow the trail of clues to locate missing persons. Even though a child, for example, may be lost, the tracker gets through to find and rescue him. In this analogy, when you think you're all alone—maybe even trying to "get lost" because of shame or guilt—God's goodness and love find you anyway and bring you back to safety.

2. One of the most dramatic—and popular—stories of God's faithfulness to a man in terrible circumstances is the account of Joseph (Gen. 37–50). What do you learn about the rivalry that existed between Joseph and his brothers in Genesis 37:2–20?

3. When the brothers plotted to kill Joseph, an event occurred (you might call it a "coincidence") that protected Joseph from death. What was it (vv. 21–28)?

4. Even though Joseph was now a slave, he ended up ("coincidentally") in a place of opportunity. What was that situation (Gen. 39:1–6)?

5. In spite of the blessing of his position, what evil happened to Joseph (vv. 7–20)?

6. After that further injustice, what blessing occurred even in prison (vv. 21–23)?

7. Joseph eventually came to the attention of Pharaoh because he interpreted a dream to the Pharaoh's chief cupbearer who had been thrown in jail two years earlier and ended up ("coincidentally") with Joseph. Now that Pharaoh had a troubling dream, the cupbearer recommended Joseph to interpret it. What was the result of that "chance" meeting and Joseph helping Pharaoh (Gen. 41:38–45)?

8. Joseph—former hated kid brother, slave, unjustly imprisoned, forgotten man—was now second in command to Pharaoh. When the famine Pharaoh dreamed about came to pass, Joseph's family was also ("coincidentally") affected, and they came to Egypt to buy grain. This contact reconnected the lost family, and Joseph was eventually reunited with his brothers and father (Gen. 46:29–30). Yet his brothers were rightfully afraid of the consequences of their sinful treatment of Joseph. How did Joseph respond to their apology (Gen. 50:15–21)?

Is Joseph excusing his brothers' behavior? What do you learn about God's ability to bring good even out of evil actions?

9. How does Romans 8:28 relate to this story?

10. What is the difference between saying "all things that happen are good" and "in all things God works for the good"?

11. Being a Christ-follower not only means good things happen *to* us, but that good things happen *through* us. As our Good Shepherd cares for us, we grow "wool" to provide for others (or, using the images of Psalm 23, our goodness and love should chase or nip at the heels of others). During the last week or so, in what ways have you been an agent of goodness and love?

TAKE-AWAY

My summary of the main point of this session, and how it impacts me personally:

> NOTE: You will fill in this information after your group discussion. Leave it blank until the conclusion of your meeting.

SESSION
SIX

Grace Forever

And I will dwell in the house of the LORD forever.

—PSALM 23:6B

Reading adapted from *In the Grip of Grace* by Max Lucado

How does God feel about me when I'm a jerk?

C an anything separate us from the love Christ has for us?" (Rom. 8:35).

There it is. This is the question. Here is what we want to know. We want to know how long God's love will endure. Does God really love us forever? Not just on Easter Sunday when our shoes are shined and our hair is fixed. How does God feel about me when I'm a jerk? Not when I'm peppy and positive and ready to tackle world hunger. Not then. I know how he feels about me then. Even I like me then.

I want to know how he feels about me when I snap at anything that moves, when my thoughts are gutter-level, when my tongue is sharp enough to slice a rock.

That's the question. That's the concern. Did I cross the line this week? Last Tuesday when I drank vodka until I couldn't walk ... last Thursday when my business took me where I had no business being ... last summer when I cursed the God who made me as I stood near the grave of the child he gave me?

Did I drift too far? Wait too long? Slip too much?

First of all, remember your position—you are a child of God. Some interpret the presence of the battle as the abandonment of God. Their logic goes something like this: "I am a Christian. My desires, however, are anything but Christian. No child of God would have these battles. I must be an orphan. God may have given me a place back then, but he has no place for me now."

That's Satan sowing those seeds of shame. If he can't seduce you with your sin, he'll let you sink in your guilt. "God's tired of your struggles," he whispers. "Your Father is weary of your petitions for forgiveness," he lies. And many believe him, spending years convinced that they are disqualified from the kingdom.

Can I go to the well of grace too many times? I don't deserve to ask for forgiveness again.

Forgive my abrupt response, but who told you that you deserved forgiveness the first time? If your sin were too great for his grace, he never would have saved you in the first place. Your temptation isn't late-breaking news in heaven. When you came to Christ he knew every sin you had committed. And he knew you would continue committing sin in the future. Your sin doesn't surprise God. He saw it coming. Is there any reason to think that the One who received you the first time won't receive you every time?

Your sin doesn't surprise God. He saw it coming.

Besides, the very fact that you are under attack must mean that you're on the right side. Did you notice who else had times of struggle? The apostle Paul did.

> *I do not understand my own actions. For I do not do what I want, but I do the very thing I hate ... I can will what is right, but I cannot do it. For I do not do the good I want, but the evil I do not want is what I do.*
>
> —Romans 7:15ff

Paul is not describing a struggle of the past, but a struggle in the present. For all we know, Paul was engaged in spiritual combat even as he wrote the letter to the Romans. *You mean the apostle Paul battled sin while he was writing a book in the Bible?* Can you think of a more strategic time for Satan to attack? Is it possible that Satan feared the fruit of this letter to the Romans?

Could it be that he fears the fruits of your life? Could it be that you are under attack—not because you are so weak but because you might become so strong? Perhaps he hopes that in defeating you today he will have one less missionary or writer or giver or singer to fight with tomorrow.

The same One who saved us first is there to save us still.

There is never a point at which you are any less saved than you were the first moment he saved you. Just because you were grumpy at breakfast doesn't mean you were condemned at breakfast. When you lost your temper yesterday, you didn't lose your salvation. Your name doesn't disappear and reappear in the book of life according to your moods and actions. Such is the message of grace. "There is now no condemnation for those who are in Christ Jesus" (Rom. 8:1).

Your name doesn't disappear and reappear in the book of life according to your moods and actions.

"You wonder how long my love will last?" Jesus asks. "Find your answer on a splintered cross, on a craggy hill. That's me you see up there, your maker, your God, nail-stabbed and bleeding. Covered in spit and sin-soaked. That's your sin I'm feeling. That's your death I'm dying. That's your resurrection I'm living. That's how much I love you."

"Can anything come between you and me?" asks the firstborn Son.

Hear the answer and stake your future on the triumphant words of Paul:

I am sure that neither death, nor life, nor angels, nor ruling spirits, nothing now, nothing in the future, no powers, nothing above us, nothing below us, nor anything else in the whole world will ever be able to separate us from the love of God that is in Christ Jesus our Lord.

—Romans 8:38–39

SPIRITUAL EXERCISE

And I will dwell in the house of the LORD forever.

—Psalm 23:6b

As you go through your week, consider the significance of the little word *forever.*

First, find ways to remind yourself of the word itself. Here are some suggestions:

- On each day of the week in your daily calendar, write "forever."
- Write "forever" on a 3 x 5 card and tape it to your bathroom mirror; put another one on the visor of your car.
- Use Post-it notes and place them around your house, on your refrigerator, on your TV, on your computer monitor (if you have a screen saver with text options, write "forever" there, too).
- Call someone in your group and leave a simple message, "Just calling to remind you: 'forever!'" Ask someone in your group to do the same for you a few times throughout the week.

Every time during the week when you see the word, remind yourself, *I will live in God's grace forever.* What does that mean to you? How does that thought comfort you, right now and each time you read it?

Forever doesn't start after death; your forever with God has already begun. So when you see the word, ask yourself, "How am I doing dwelling in God's house right now?" Every meal, every activity, when you lay down or rise up, it is all being done in his presence, in his name. He is already on your side, wanting to be close to you, and all of this will be true forever.

Consider keeping a "dwelling in the house" journal through the day. At various intervals (say, once every few hours) note on a scale of 1–10 the degree to which you are feeling loved by and at home with the Father. Also note whatever seems to rob you of that feeling. What enhances it? Do you see any patterns in your experience?

This week will be one to remember—*forever.*

1. Even in the midst of opposition, loss, and personal failure, David had a profound sense of security. It was rooted in the reality that he would dwell with his God—and his God would dwell with him—every day on earth and every day in eternity. The apostle Paul echoed that same sense of deep security in Romans 8. While David uses the picture of sheep being cared for by a shepherd, Paul makes a different analogy. What image does he use in Romans 8:15–17?

NOTE: The word *abba* is Aramaic for daddy—a much more intimate and affectionate name than the term father. It was somewhat unusual for Jesus to call God Father; it was absolutely radical to call him "Daddy." Yet Paul says the Holy Spirit moves in us to create this kind of intimate relationship with the God of the universe.

What does the image Paul chose say about the security of your position in Christ?

2. Paul candidly addresses the fear of condemnation that accompanied his own battle with sin (Rom. 7:18–25). Recently, how have you felt the fear of condemnation?

How have you dealt with that?

3. According to 2 Corinthians 7:8–10, what is the difference between being appropriately convicted of sin and feeling condemned?

4. Look at Romans 8:1 and 33. How would your life be different if you really believed this to the core of your being?

5. Imagine charges being brought to the throne of God concerning you—an exposé of all those things you wish you could keep hidden. According to Romans 8:34, what specific role does Jesus play day in and day out with respect to those charges?

Expand on this picture of Jesus as your lawyer [which is one way to understand the role of intercessor; in I John 2:1–2 [NRSV], he is actually called our "advocate"). What does this mean for you in your daily life as a Christian?

6. Romans 8:35 describes other possible barriers to God's love. What experiences or feelings periodically shake your sense of security or make you feel separated from the love of Christ?

7. Think of a time in your life when someone stood up for you or strongly supported you. What did that person do? How did you feel about that person being *for* you?

What does it mean to say that "God is for us" (Rom. 8:31)? Give a specific example of how he is—or has been—for *you*.

8. Read about the church of Laodicea in Revelation 3:14–17. Note that security misunderstood can lead to some harmful attitudes or actions—carelessness, complacency, or taking the relationship for granted. How can you keep this from happening as you increasingly learn to live in the security of God's grace?

9. Paraphrase Paul's words in Romans 8:35 and 38–39, listing those things that are most personal for you.

TAKE-AWAY

My summary of the main point of this session, and how it impacts me personally:

> NOTE: You will fill in this information after your group discussion. Leave it blank until the conclusion of your meeting.

SESSION
SEVEN

GRACE TO SHARE

Grace to Share

I have other sheep that are not of this sheep pen. I must bring them also. They too will listen to my voice, and there shall be one flock and one shepherd.

—JOHN 10:16

Reading adapted from a message by Bill Hybels

"We're not doing right. This is a day of good news and we are keeping it to ourselves."

Hundreds of years before Christ, the ancient city of Samaria was besieged by an enemy king, Ben-Hadad. Ben-Hadad's plan was simple: surround the city with troops, cutting the people off from all resources, including food. The people would starve. Victory would be easily achieved.

The plan was working. The famine was taking its toll. Donkey heads, dove dung—virtually anything that could be ingested, people ate. Parents were even boiling their very own children for food! Things were as bad as they could get.

Four lepers stood at the gate of the city, clinging—barely—to life. They considered their options. They could go into the city and starve. They could stay where they were and die. Or they could take a risk and go to the camp of the enemy hoping maybe—just maybe—the soldiers would have pity and throw them a few scraps. Together they reasoned, "If they kill us—then we die" (2 Kings 7:4).

The lepers set out timidly from the city gate. But as they approached the enemy camp something seemed wrong. There was no activity. The camp was deserted! God had ambushed the enemy with the sound of chariots and horses, and they had fled, leaving everything behind.

The lepers couldn't believe their good fortune. They entered tent after tent, eating and drinking. There was enough food and drink to feed an army—literally! Soon they began stockpiling—carrying off silver, gold, clothes, and provisions and hiding them.

But in the dark with bellies full, they started having second thoughts. "We're not doing right. This is a day of good news and we are keeping it to ourselves. . . . Let's go at once and report this to the royal palace" (v. 9). The lepers return to Samaria to report what they found. The story ends with the people of the city flooding the camp. The famine ended that very night.

An evangelistic lifestyle is most certainly the will of Jesus and most certainly worth the risks involved.

Taking a Risk

Let me share a few things I love about this story. First, I love the lepers' go-for-broke attitude. I love the way they size up their situation. They do a quick cost-benefit analysis. In effect they ask, "What's the worst thing that could happen to us if we go for it? We could die." With the upside being life itself, they decide it's worth the risk. They roll the dice.

I can't help but see a parallel with living a contagious Christian life. Do you know when an individual Christian really begins the adventure of reaching out to other sheep not yet of this fold? It is when it dawns on the person that an evangelistic lifestyle is most certainly the will of Jesus and most certainly worth the risks involved. It is when a person does that cost-benefit analysis and asks, "What is the absolute worst thing that could happen if I start getting more intentional about sharing my faith?"

I'll tell you what the worst thing is, in this country anyway: someone might decline your effort. Someone may say, "I'm not ready to take that step," or even, "Thanks, but no thanks." In this country, that's just about as bloody as it's going to get. I ask you, is that really so awful?

Some of us are so paralyzed by the possibility of rejection, of someone saying, "Thanks, but no thanks," that we have fallen into a well-developed pattern of never trying, never risking.

Do you remember Jesus' parable of the sower and the seed? The sower is out there sowing seed faithfully. Some of it falls on hard ground and never takes root. It's a bust. Some falls on rocky soil. Another bust. Some falls on thorny soil. Ultimately, that's a bust too. Bust, bust, bust. But then Jesus says that some falls on good soil, takes root, and changes everything.

Why did Jesus tell this story? To tell his followers, "Don't give up! Keep sowing the seed—again and again and again. You will get 'busts' and your heart will get broken. But you will hear the whisper of God saying, 'But you *tried. Well done!'"* And there will be an esteem in your spirit knowing that at least you were a faithful witness. Who knows, the seed you sowed might germinate later. Maybe your role was just to loosen the hard-packed soil.

People don't tend to come to Christ until an ordinary Christian like you or me gets in the game.

The main point is this: People don't tend to come to Christ until an ordinary Christian like you or me gets in the game and asks the question, "What is the worst possible downside in sharing Christ with this person? I may experience the sting of rejection. Possible upside? Eternity!"

Delighting in the Stockpile

Another thing I love about the story is the extent to which the lepers drank in their good fortune. I can just picture those starving lepers sampling every kind of food they could get their hands on, trying on clothes, laughing, handling the jewelry and rings—just having a ball! I think they felt complete freedom to get their fill of everything there.

In the same way, the most effective ambassadors of the love of Christ over the long haul are those who have given themselves full permission to drink in the lavishness of

God's grace. You show me someone who drinks in spiritual blessings with great liberality, and I'll show you someone who is spilling over with the desire to tell others how it is available.

On the other hand, show me a Christian who is locked into legalism, into a joyless, performance-oriented Christianity, and I'll show you someone who isn't very fired up about inviting their best friends into that kind of life.

This is why it is so critical for us all to be pursuing a life rich in celebration, joy, satisfying relationships—and to have fun! Because when you're filled up, you are more likely to invite others to share in the stockpile of God's grace.

Sharing from the Stockpile

Show me someone who drinks in spiritual blessings with great liberality, and I'll show you someone who is spilling over with the desire to tell others how it is available.

This leads us back to the story. All of a sudden, while the lepers are trying on clothes and eating and drinking, they remember the people in the city, who are still eating donkey heads and dove dung! They realize it's unconscionable not to share the news of the stockpile with the others!

The parallel is obvious. We are learning to ask the question, "What would Jesus do if he were in my place?" Putting it another way, "What would it be like to have Jesus' eyes for just one hour?"

Jesus always saw people through redemptive lenses. When Jesus looked at a group of people, he would say, "There's a person I'm crazy about. There's another one I'm crazy about. There's *another* one I'm crazy about!" He knows each person is a prayer away from moving from darkness to light, from isolation to community, from hell to heaven forever. It's impossible for him to look at a person *without* the desire to bring them to the stockpile of God's grace.

This is why Jesus' final word to his followers was "Go!" Go into your schools, your neighborhoods, your marketplace. Go into the inner city, the neighboring nations, and all over the world. Take a risk. Let go of fear. Sow seed!

Can you imagine the lepers standing off to the side while tens of thousands of starved people crawled on their hands and knees finding food, drink, clothing, dishes, silverware? Can you imagine how filled up they were with a sense of God's lavish grace? Can you imagine the inner affirmation they felt? They took a risk and it paid off. They shared what they could have hoarded. They did the *right thing*.

May that be true about us!

1. Read Luke 15. What are the common themes of these three stories?

Why do you think Jesus uses three stories to get his point across?

NOTE: Listen to what *The Journey, a Bible for Seeking God and Understanding Life* has to say about these three stories:

Most people find it hard to identify with lost sheep. But a lost dog? Now that's a different story. If Jesus were to tell the parable of the lost sheep today, he might make it the parable of the lost dog. The idea is the same. If your dog runs off, you search for it until you find it. And when you bring it home your family celebrates.

The next story deserves a bit of historical illumination. Palestinian women traditionally received a set of 10 coins as a wedding gift. These coins were either carried around in a purse or on a chain, and held similar significance to a modern-day wedding ring. No wonder this woman would search so fervently to find the

> *lost coin, and no wonder she would want to celebrate upon find-*
> *ing it!*
>
> *We don't have to stretch too far to understand the third story.*
> *Imagine that you're a parent and that your son leaves home with*
> *as much money as he can pull together. He departs for a big city*
> *like New York, Los Angeles, or San Francisco. After he blows*
> *every cent he has on drugs, sex, and alcohol, he ends up on the*
> *street.*
>
> *As his parents, you wait for the day he'll come home. Every time*
> *the phone rings or you hear a car outside, you hope it's him. One*
> *day you open the front door, and there he stands! Instantly you*
> *throw your arms around him. Words can't express the joy you*
> *feel. Your son who was lost is home!*
>
> *These three stories express how God feels about every seeker.*

2. It's very clear that God sought us out—Jesus living among us
    is the best example of this. We are the lost sheep, coins, and
    children he came to rescue. In John 17:18, Jesus prayed to the
    Father, "As you sent me into the world, I have sent them into
    the world." To live as if Jesus were in our place means bring-
    ing grace to *other* lost people, just as he did. As you consider
    your own life, what are some barriers right now that hinder you
    from doing that effectively?

3. In Colossians 4:3–6, why is Paul so urgent about sharing the gospel? (See also Eph. 5:15–16.)

Though our circumstances may be different than Paul's (we are not in prison for being Christians), what timeless principles concerning evangelism come through this passage?

4. Take some time to reflect on your own stockpile—all the blessings that God's grace has brought to you. Under each category of blessings listed below (which are based on the sessions of this study), write down specific events, people, or provisions that demonstrate each kind of grace in your life. (Look back over the particular session indicated if you need help remembering.) When you have completed each section, think of some physical object that symbolizes that kind of grace overall for you. It could be the actual item (such as a gift from a relative who had a great impact on you) or a symbol (a toy car that represents a car accident you survived). In some cases, you may need to write a word or phrase on a piece of paper to represent that aspect of God's kindness. Collect these six items together— they are your stockpile—and bring them to your next small group meeting. Be prepared to tell briefly the story behind each item, and why it symbolizes that particular kind of grace in your life.

Session 1: Grace That Comes in Ordinary Moments

Symbol of this for me:

Session 2: Grace That Forgives Me

Symbol of this for me:

Session 3: Grace That Sustains Me Through Hard Times

Symbol of this for me:

Session 4: Grace That Brings Me Joy

Symbol of this for me:

Session 5: Grace That Helps Me Build a Legacy

Symbol of this for me:

Symbol of this for me:

5. Read the account of the Ethiopian's conversion in Acts 8:26–39. Who has God used in your life to lead *you* to this stockpile of grace—someone who shared the gospel or helped answer your spiritual questions? Describe the significance or impact of that person.

It is easy to forget that everyone you meet is someone with whom God may want you to have a ministry, maybe even to be instrumental in their coming to Christ. What if you had eyes every day to see people as Jesus sees them? Not as interruptions but as divine appointments; not as irritants but as lost sheep in need of a shepherd. We all need "redemptive lenses" to help us when we make those daily, split-second judgments—"spiritual glasses" to help us see people as he sees them. Along those lines, here are some steps to try this week to help you become more effective in bringing others to the stockpile. As you go about your activities, replay the following questions and see what God does!

Noticing

Who are some people in my world who perhaps don't know God yet? Who might I be overlooking?

Praying

Who could I put on my prayer list of those I desire to meet Christ? What object in my house, office, or on the road to work could serve as a reminder to pray for those people?

Taking a Relational Step

What is one thing I can do this week to draw closer and express love to someone who does not yet know God?

Verbal Witness

What is one comment I might make or question I might ask that could steer a conversation toward spiritual matters?

Taking a Risk

What challenge or invitation could I give to encourage someone to take the next step in his or her spiritual life?

TAKE-AWAY

My summary of the main point of this session, and how it impacts me personally:

NOTE: You will fill in this information after your group discussion. Leave it blank until the conclusion of your meeting.

Leader's Guide

How to Use This Discussion Guide

Doers of the Word

One of the reasons small groups are so effective is because when people are face-to-face, they can discuss and process information instead of merely listening passively. *God's truths are transforming only to the extent they are received and absorbed.* Just as uneaten food cannot nourish, truth "out there"—either in a book or spoken by a teacher—cannot make a difference if it is undigested. Even if it is bitten off and chewed, it must be swallowed and made part of each cell to truly give life.

The spiritual transformation at the heart of this Bible study series can occur only if people get truth and make that truth part of their lives. Reading about sit-ups leaves you flabby; doing sit-ups gives you strong abdominals. That's why in every session, we present group members with exercises to do during the week. They also study Scripture on their own in (hopefully) unhurried settings where they can meditate on and ponder the truths that are encountered. Group discussion is the other way we've designed for them to grab hold of these important lessons.

This study is not a correspondence course. It's a personal and group experience designed to help believers find a biblical approach to their spiritual lives that really works. We recognize that people have a variety of learning styles, so we've tried to incorporate a variety of ways to learn. One of the most important ways they will learn is when they meet together to process the information verbally in a group.

Not Question-by-Question

One approach to learning used by some small groups encourages members to systematically discuss *everything* they learn on their own during the group time. Such material is designed so group members do a study and then report what their answers were for each question. While this approach is thorough, it can become boring. The method we've adopted includes individual study, but we do not suggest discussing *everything* in the session when you meet. Instead, questions are given to leaders (hence, this Leader's Guide) to get at the heart of the material without being rote recitations of the answers the members came up with on their own. This may be a bit confusing at first, because some people fill in the blanks, expecting each answer to be discussed, and discussed in the order they wrote them down. Instead, you, as a leader, will be asking questions *based* on their study, but not necessarily numerically corresponding to their study. We think this technique of handling the sessions has the best of both approaches: individual learning is reinforced in the group setting without becoming wearisome.

It is also important that you understand you will not be able to cover all the material provided each week. We give you more than you can use in every session—not to frustrate you, but to give you enough so you can pick and choose. *Base your session plan on the needs of individual members of your group.*

There may be a few times when the material is so relevant to your group members that every question seems to fit. Don't feel bad about taking two weeks on a session. The purpose of this series is transformational life-change, not timely book completion!

Getting Ready for *Your* Group

We suggest that to prepare for a meeting, you first do the study yourself and spend some time doing the spiritual exercise. Then look over the questions we've given you in the Leader's Guide. As you consider your group members and the amount of discussion time you have, ask yourself if the questions listed for that session relate to your group's needs. Would some other questions fit better? We've tried to highlight the main points of each session, but you may feel you need to hit some aspect harder than we did, or not spend as much time on a point. As long as your preparation is based on knowledge of your group, customize the session however you see fit.

As we pointed out, you may have to adapt the material because of time considerations. It is very hard to discuss every topic in a given session in detail—we certainly don't recommend it. You may also only have a limited time because of the nature of your group. Again, the purpose isn't to cover every question exhaustively, but to get the main point across in each session (whatever incidental discussion may otherwise occur). As a guide to your preparation, review the *Primary Focus* statement at the beginning and the *Session Highlights* paragraph at the end of each session's Leader's Guide. They represent our attempt to summarize what we were trying to get across in writing the sessions. If your questions get at those points, you're on the right track.

A Guide, Not a Guru

Now a word about your role as leader. We believe all small groups need a leader. While it is easy to see that a group discussion would get off track without a facilitator, we would like you to ponder another very important reason you hold the position you do.

This Bible study series is about spiritual growth—about Christ being formed in each of us. One of the greatest gifts you can give another person is to pay attention to his or her spiritual life. As a leader, you will serve your group members by observing their lives and trying to hear, in the questions they ask and the answers they give, where they are in their spiritual development. Your discerning observations are an invaluable contribution to their spiritual progress. That attention, prayer, and insight is an extremely rare gift—but it is revolutionary for those blessed enough to have such a person in their lives. You are that person. You give that gift. You can bring that blessing.

People desperately need clarity about spirituality. Someone needs to blow away the fog that surrounds the concept of what it means to live a spiritual life and give believers concrete ideas how to pursue it. Spiritual life is just *life*. It's that simple. Christ-followers must invite God into all aspects of life, even the everyday routines. That is where we spend most of our time anyway, so that is where we must be with God. If not, the Christian life will become pretense, or hypocrisy. We must decompartmentalize life so that we share it all with God in a barrier-free union with him.

We say all this so that you, the leader, can be encouraged in and focused on your role. You are the person observing how people are doing. You are the one who detects the doors people will not let God through, the one who sees the blind spots they don't, the one who gently points out the unending patience of God who will not stop working in us until "his work is completed" (Phil. 1:6). You will hold many secret conversations with God about the people in your group—while you meet, during a phone call, sitting across the table at lunch, when you're alone. In addition to making the meeting happen, this is one of the most important things you can do to be a catalyst for life-change. That is why you're meeting together anyway—to see people become more like Christ. If you lead as a *facilitator* of discussion, not a teacher, and a *listener* rather than the one who should be listened to, you will see great changes in the members of your group.

Living in Grace

Primary Focus: To learn how to recognize and experience grace in everyday life.

Remember that these questions do not correspond numerically with the questions in the assignment. We do not recommend simply going over what your group members put for their answers—that will probably result in a tedious discussion at best. Rather, use these questions (and perhaps some of your own) to stimulate discussion: that way, you'll be processing the content of the lesson from a fresh perspective each meeting.

1. How did you do with the challenge to practice the discipline of noticing? What is your biggest barrier to living this way on a consistent basis?

2. Share with the group one or two examples of God's "ordinary grace" that you tend to take for granted, but this week you had eyes to see. What connection did you discover between noticing and experiencing grace?

3. Are there any special ways God led you to "green pastures and still waters" during the past week? Were you able to really "lie down" and receive his refreshment?

4. *(Regarding question 4 in the Bible study)* We know sheep often resist rest. What most often keeps you from resting?

5. *(Regarding question 7 in the Bible study)* How would you describe your contentment quotient right now? Do you find yourself more settled or more wanting these days?

6. *(Regarding question 7 in the Bible study)* How can you be genuine with God about your needs and desires while still cultivating a contented spirit?

NOTE: God takes great delight when his children come openly to him with needs and even their everyday desires. He repeatedly tells us to ask (Phil. 4:6; James 4:2; Heb. 4:16). But when we move from asking to demanding—when we start focusing on what he hasn't done instead of what he has and is doing—that's a problem! Contentment doesn't come from always getting your desires; it comes from trusting that your Shepherd knows your real needs and what he gives you is enough for today.

7. *(Regarding question 6 in the Bible study)* What soul restoring would you like your Shepherd to do right now? What steps can you take to create the conditions for that to happen? Is there any way we, as a group, can help?

8. *(Regarding question 8 in the Bible study)* What are the greatest barriers in your life that keep you from seeing God as a green-pasture-loving, still-water-giving, soul-restoring Shepherd?

Take-Away: At the conclusion of your discussion each week, take a few minutes to have group members sum up the session and its impact on them by filling in the Take-Away section at the end of each session. Don't tell them what they are supposed to write—let them be true to their own experiences. When they have written their summaries, have everyone share with the others what they wrote. Statements should be similar to the statements in Session Highlights. If you feel the whole group may have missed an important aspect of the session, be sure to bring that up in the closing discussion.

Session Highlights: God is my intimate Shepherd and wants to pour his grace into every area of my life; I need to train myself to notice it, experience it, and be restored by it.

NOTE: In the next session, the spiritual exercise follows the Bible study and requires setting aside a block of time to engage in personal review and confession. We suggest you alert your group members so that they allow enough time to complete the exercise.

SESSION TWO

Grace for Regrets

Primary Focus: To learn how to practice confession in order to experience God's forgiveness more deeply.

1. *(Regarding question 1 in the Bible study)* What makes hiding such a natural response to sin? How does hiding sabotage living in grace?

2. Certainly, God already knows all the details concerning our sin. So why is it important to be specific in confession? How difficult is that for you?

> NOTE: "Glossing" is really just another way of hiding—being so general in our confession that we can avoid the sting of embarrassment and owning up. Real growth is much more likely to occur when we clearly identify our disobedience and take responsibility for it.

3. Have you been able to identify any ways in which you are trying to meet legitimate needs in illegitimate ways? What are some ways you could meet those needs honorably?

4. *(Regarding question 5 in the Bible study)* Why is trying hard to earn forgiveness as well as groveling in despair pointless when it comes to living in grace?

5. By the end of the exercise, did you feel the reality of grace? If not, what do you think would have helped? As a final step of confession, what do you see as the pros and cons of sharing your confession with a mature Christian friend?

6. *(Regarding question 7 in the Bible study)* How can the truth of God's forgiveness "for his name's sake" enrich your walk with him?

NOTE: If someone is having a hard time feeling grace and forgiveness, you may consider taking some time as a group to read through some of the forgiveness passages included in the session (or others that are your favorites).

During the discussion, someone may end up sharing openly about a sensitive personal matter. While this is a great step for the person, additional follow-up from you, the leader, may be in order. A phone call the next day would probably be a great encouragement. Let the person know you are committed to walking alongside as he or she continues in his or her process; offer accountability if that is appropriate. You may want to suggest additional resources, such as Max Lucado's *In the Grip of Grace*, Lewis Smedes' *Shame and Grace*, or William Backus' *Telling Yourself the Truth*. Most important of all is simply showing God's grace in action through your ongoing concern and support.

Close in a time of prayer, lifting up those who are particularly struggling with forgiveness and grace. Speak words of blessing, grounded in the promises of God's Word, that grace is readily available. We are already forgiven based on what Christ has done for us; as a leader, speak that truth to your group members as you pray, and thank God for its reality.

Session Highlights: I don't need to run from God in shame; confession is a gracious bridge from regrets to healing and transformation.

SESSION THREE

Sustaining Grace

Primary Focus: To learn to "bet the farm" on God's grace.

> NOTE: Even more than other weeks, the goal this week is not to work through all the questions but to provide a safe setting where group members can openly share and reflect on current "valleys" in their own lives. Use the questions just as needed to help people talk about their experiences. Also, we are suggesting a time of guided prayer at the end allowing members to join supportively with one another amidst the valley.

1. The reading alluded to one of Bill Hybels' own "dark valley" experiences. What is it for you these days that most often makes you feel fearful or is pressing you to your limit? (Encourage people to share as specifically or as generally as they are comfortable doing.)

2. Describe some of the feelings you've been experiencing concerning your point of pressure or pain. How much emotional energy are you regularly expending regarding it?

3. Is there any way in which you have been tempted to pursue a man-made way out, a "Plan B," a way of doing pain management that is not God's idea or plan?

4. To what extent have you felt (or not felt) your Shepherd's presence—his "strong support"—in this valley?

5. What passages of Scripture most strengthened you?

6. This study is ultimately about spiritual transformation—growing to know Christ more intimately and to live each day as he would live it. Is there any way you see this happening specifically through your experiences of pain and difficulty? How is your Shepherd changing you even in the valley?

Guided Prayer: Allow extra time at the end of the meeting to supportively pray for one another. You might have each group member pray out loud for the person to his or her right—and even commit to continue praying for that person throughout the week.

After everyone has prayed, you should close the time of prayer. Consider including an opportunity to make a "trusting covenant" together. For example, you could pray:

"Lord, in the midst of these valleys, we come to you as our Good Shepherd. Help each of us sense and feel that you are with us, especially in the darkness. Even as we wrestle with those things causing us pain, pressure, or anxiety, we want to covenant together, as best we can, to trust you alone. Right now, we are holding on to your promise that you will strongly support those whose hearts are completely yours. Now, Lord, help us to leave in peace, with the reminder that our strong and gracious Shepherd goes with us. Amen."

Session Highlights: God will take me through every valley of the shadow of death; my "Plan B" is never as good as God's will for me; I must choose to rely on God's sustaining grace.

SESSION FOUR

Delighting in Grace

Primary Focus: To learn to practice celebration in order to become a more joyful person.

> NOTE: Use this week as an opportunity to celebrate as a group. Try finding a way to celebrate in a style that is consistent with who your group is. Maybe you could meet in a new location (forest preserve, restaurant, zoo, park, etc.), or add some surprises to the meeting. Below are some possibilities.

- Surprise everyone with a small gift (maybe give everyone a small frame, and then get your picture taken as a group, or give a tape, a book, or a note of affirmation).
- Take turns listening to everyones favorite music.
- Buy or prepare special food (a favorite pie, tray of fresh fruit, order some pizza, or maybe have an entire celebration dinner).
- Share, one at a time, the best celebration you've ever been a part of.
- Watch a football game together.
- Have a meal at a special restaurant and go over your lesson there.

1. How did the exercise go? How difficult was it to live in joy for a full week? What was one highlight? To what extent did you have to exercise "nevertheless joy"?

2. What did you discern regarding your tendencies with respect to joy? Are you more lighthearted by nature, such that enjoying life comes quite easily? Or do you tend to be more on the serious side, so celebration and joy comes with some difficulty?

3. What do you think contributed to the development of these tendencies? (Family background? Understanding of God? Just the way you're wired up?)

4. If you tend toward the lighthearted side, how do you keep the pursuit of joy and pleasure from becoming selfish or even sinful?

NOTE: You may need to clarify for people how they can know when joy is God-honoring pleasure. For instance, it:

- is consistent with Scripture
- leaves you with a clean conscience
- draws you toward God, not away from God
- leads to the generous extension of joy and grace to others (not to self-absorbed pleasure-seeking)

5. If you tend toward the more serious side, why is it important for you to grow in the area of joy and celebration?

NOTE: Possible answers:

- Joy is God's intent for you.
- Because joy "seasons" your witness to nonbelievers.
- Joy is strength.

6. How did you react to the concept that "joy is strength" (as stated in the reading)?

7. How can the absence of joy actually weaken us in our ability to live godly lives?

8. *(Regarding question 7 in the Bible study)* Have you gotten a little soul-weary or joyless of late? If so, what do you think it will take to start reversing this pattern?

9. *(Regarding question 8 in the Bible study)* What do you think about the "sanctified partying" commanded by God? Does this affect your view of God in any way? How easy is it for you to imagine God saying, "Pick your favorite activity and let's enjoy it together"?

Session Highlights: Joy is a part of God's purpose for my life. Joy is a strength. Legitimate pleasures are means of grace.

A Word about Leadership: Remember the comments at the beginning of this discussion guide about your role as a leader? About now, it's probably a good idea to remind yourself that one of your key functions is to be a cheerleader—someone who seeks out signs of spiritual progress in others and makes some noise about it.

What have you seen God doing in your group members' lives as a result of this study? Don't assume that they've seen that progress—and definitely don't assume they are beyond needing simple words of encouragement. Find ways to point out to people the growth you've seen. Let them know it's happening, and that it's noticeable to you and others.

There aren't a whole lot of places in this world where people's spiritual progress is going to be recognized and celebrated. After all, wouldn't you like to hear someone cheer you on? So would your group members. You have the power to make a profound impact through a sincere, insightful remark.

Be aware, also, that some groups get sidetracked by a difficult member or situation that hasn't been confronted. And some individuals *could* be making significant progress—they just need a nudge. Encouragement is not about just saying nice things; it's about offering *words that urge*. It's about giving courage (en-*courage*-ment) to those who lack it.

So, take a risk. Say what needs to be said to encourage your members toward their goal of becoming fully devoted followers.

A Legacy of Grace

Primary Focus: To see God's abundant grace and desire to be gracious in response.

1. In reviewing the eras of your life, what did you observe about the way God's goodness and love have personally followed you? (If time permits, ask each person to share one high point and one low point.)

2. What is the difference between saying "all things that happen are good" and "in all things God works for the good"? How was this illustrated in the life of Joseph? How has it been illustrated throughout the eras of your own life?

> NOTE: It is certainly true that we don't know in the midst of life experiences just exactly how God is going to turn some evil into good. We need to be sensitive about how we talk about God's sovereignty, especially to those in the midst of pain. It's okay not to have neat and tidy answers to all the whys and wherefores of someone's crisis. The good that God eventually is going to do may not be clear at all; there's no point pretending to know what hasn't come to pass yet. Only in heaven will some questions get their full answer. We trust God not because the good is visible but even though it isn't yet.

3. What impact should this legacy of God's goodness have on your anxiety level as you experience present and future valleys?

4. Goodness and grace follow us not only through the major events and eras of our lives but also throughout the moments of our days. To what extent were you able to experience this through the exercise? When was God's goodness and love most easy for you to feel? When was it most difficult?

5. Now consider your own legacy. Do goodness and love follow you in your wake? Share one or two good things you left behind this week. Were there any times when you feel you failed in this endeavor?

> NOTE: Be sure to emphasize the positive here. Your role as a leader is to catch people doing the right things, not shame them for their unfinished work If someone has a hard time coming up with something, have the group members fill in the blanks for each other. As the leader, come up with something for each of your group members before the meeting so you can add to what is said when you get to this question.

6. Did you extend grace to anyone outside your normal sphere of relating—perhaps to someone of a different ethnic, cultural, or economic group? What was that experience like?

> NOTE: Possible "Grace Extension" Experience. Our goal in spiritual formation is to walk as Jesus would walk if in our place. Having been recipients of his lavish grace, we are to be extenders of it. Throughout his life, Jesus had particular concern that grace be extended to those deemed unlovable, poor, "different," on the fringes of society (Matt. 25:31–46).
>
> This would be a great opportunity to stretch your group with a "grace extension" experience—a time when your entire group would commit to serving for a day together in an under-resourced community. Check with your church or other local organizations for opportunities. This could be a life-changing, heart-changing group event!

Session Highlights: When I take the time to look, I will see God's grace throughout my life; I need to be intentional about extending grace to others.

SESSION SIX

Grace Forever

Primary Focus: To rest secure in God's grace forever.

1. What most frequently makes you feel insecure in your relationship with God? Do you ever experience the fear of condemnation—the fear that you've gone to the well of grace too many times or that it is no longer available to you?

2. In what way were Max Lucado's words an encouragement to you?

3. Was there anything specific in the Bible study that helped you move toward a deeper sense of security?

NOTE: God's intent since the beginning of history was to create a group, a people to "live in his house"—to love and be loved, to know real, eternal community with him and with each other. God's dream was shattered with the Fall, and sin has thwarted it every day through every century since—for sin is the destroyer of community. Sin separates. But God, in his grace, determined that his dream would prevail. And so he sent his Son—Jesus, the Good Shepherd—to take on our sin, to stand in the gap of separation, to open the doors of his Father's house to us.

---

4. How easy was it for you to dwell in God's house through the week? To what extent did you increase your ability to feel at home with the Father? What enhanced that ability? What hindered it? Are you able to discern any patterns?

5. *(Regarding question 5 in the Bible study)* How do you react to the picture of Jesus as your defense attorney?

6. *(Regarding question 7 in the Bible study)* What did it feel like in your past when someone stood up for you? How has God stood up for you in a way you actually feel?

7. *(Regarding question 9 in the Bible study)* Close the time together by asking each group member to read their personalized paraphrase of Romans 8:35, 38–39.

Session Highlights: If I am a Christian, nothing can separate me from God's grace; Jesus Christ will always be for me; I can rest secure in God's grace for all time.

NOTE: In the final session the Bible study and spiritual exercise are combined and include a creative way for individuals to review and memorialize the many dimensions of God's grace in their lives. Your final group meeting for this study will be based on the "objects" they select to symbolize God's grace. We suggest you review the final session and alert your members to it.

SESSION SEVEN

Grace to Share

Primary Focus: To feel and act on the urgency to extend God's grace to others.

NOTE: The final meeting is designed around a creative reflection, prayer, and worship experience—as the group literally builds their "stockpile" of grace. You will have to determine how much time to allow for each person to share, given the size of your group and length of your meeting time. It would be a good idea to give some thought to this in advance, so you don't get too rushed toward the end. It is important to finish the exercise—to get to the part where group members consider others they want to bring to the stockpile of grace. Also, if someone comes unprepared, without objects, just ask them to share verbally and then write their responses on a piece of paper and add it to the pile.

Start the meeting with one final reading together of the Twenty-third Psalm. Consider assigning one verse to each member of the group. (By now, some may have it memorized.) Recite the psalm aloud, thoughtfully and slowly.

1. *(Regarding question 4 in the Bible study)* Tonight we are going to worship our Shepherd as we build a visual reminder of the stockpile of grace that he has built for each of us. Start with the first category: "Grace that Comes in Ordinary Moments." Go around the circle and have each person place their symbolic object on the stockpile, briefly telling the story behind it—perhaps how this aspect of grace became more real to them during this study.

After each person has made a contribution to the stockpile for that category, proceed in the same manner through each category until there is a visibly abundant stockpile of grace in front of the group.

Now, lead the group through the following guided reflection time. (You may suggest that they close their eyes in order to reflect without distraction.)

Imagine right now, that standing beside the stockpile is your gracious Shepherd. Imagine his eyes looking at you with great love. Imagine his expression of great delight—like a parent's delight watching his child open gifts on Christmas morning.

Allow yourself to be still for a moment and really live with the thought that all of these gifts were prepared and personalized with just you in mind.

Now listen to these words of Paul from Ephesians 3:17–19: ". . . I pray that you, being rooted and established in love, may have power, together with all the saints, to grasp how wide and long and high and deep is the love of Christ, and to know this love that surpasses knowledge—that you may be filled to the measure of all the fullness of God."

Invite the group to spend a few moments worshiping God and expressing (silently or aloud) gratitude for the stockpile of his grace in their lives.

When appropriate, continue with the time of guided reflection . . .

Listen again to the words of the four lepers: "This is a day of good news and we are keeping it to ourselves. . . . Let's go at once and report this to [the people]."

Bring to mind some people in your world who do not know Christ: a family member, coworker, neighbor, waitress, bank teller, someone you don't even know by name but who you see often around town. Someone you like a lot . . . and someone you honestly don't care that much for.

Now imagine seeing each one through the Shepherd's eyes—through lenses of grace.

Imagine extending yourself to these individuals—asking God to show you how.

Imagine yourself taking a risk, stepping out of your comfort zone however he leads.

Imagine taking each of these people to the stockpile and to the Shepherd standing beside it.

Prayer: Close this time (and this entire study) by leading the group in a final prayer.

Include in your prayer these thoughts:

That we would continue to live in grace—to notice it, bask in it, be filled up by it, find strength in it, worship God for it.

That we would slow down and pause enough during our days to allow the Lord to be our Shepherd—through the difficult moments, the mundane moments, the joy-filled moments—through our mountaintops and dark valleys.

That goodness and grace would follow us. That we would increasingly be people marked by kindness, generosity, goodness, patience, and love.

That we would grow to see people through Jesus' eyes—that we would step out, take risks, go for broke in our efforts to lead others to the stockpile of his grace.

These are, of course, just suggestions. By all means, include whatever the Spirit lays on your heart.

Session Highlights: God is the original "seeker" who sought me first; his abundant stockpile of grace in my life motivates me to want to seek others.

John C. Ortberg Jr. is teaching pastor at Willow Creek Community Church in South Barrington, Illinois. He is the author of *The Life You've Always Wanted* and *Love Beyond Reason*. John and his wife, Nancy, live in the Chicago area with their three children, Laura, Mallory, and Johnny.

Laurie Pederson, a real estate investment manager, is a founding member of Willow Creek Community Church. As an elder since 1978, she has helped shape many of the foundational values and guiding principles of the church. She is cocreator of Willow Creek's discipleship-based church membership process. Laurie lives outside of Chicago with her husband, Scott.

Judson Poling, a staff member at Willow Creek Community Church since 1980, writes small group training materials and many of the dramas performed in Willow Creek's outreach services. He is coauthor of the *Walking with God* and *Tough Questions* Bible study series and general editor of *The Journey: A Study Bible for Spiritual Seekers*. He lives in Algonquin, Illinois, with his wife, Deb, and their two children, Anna and Ryan.

WILLOW
Willow Creek Association

Willow Creek Association
Vision, Training, Resources for Prevailing Churches

This resource was created to serve you and to help you build a local church that prevails. It is just one of many ministry tools that are part of the Willow Creek Resources® line, published by the Willow Creek Association together with Zondervan.

The Willow Creek Association (WCA) was created in 1992 to serve a rapidly growing number of churches from across the denominational spectrum that are committed to helping unchurched people become fully devoted followers of Christ. Membership in the WCA now numbers over 10,000 Member Churches worldwide from more than ninety denominations.

The Willow Creek Association links like-minded Christian leaders with each other and with strategic vision, training, and resources in order to help them build prevailing churches designed to reach their redemptive potential. Here are some of the ways the WCA does that.

- **Prevailing Church Conference**—an annual two-and-a-half day event, held at Willow Creek Community Church in South Barrington, Illinois, to help pioneering church leaders raise up a volunteer core while discovering new and innovative ways to build prevailing churches that reach unchurched people.

- **Leadership Summit**—a once-a-year, two-and-a-half-day conference to envision and equip Christians with leadership gifts and responsibilities. Presented live at Willow Creek as well as via satellite broadcast to over sixty locations across North America, this event is designed to increase the leadership effectiveness of pastors, ministry staff, volunteer church leaders, and Christians in the marketplace.

- **Ministry-Specific Conferences**—throughout each year the WCA hosts a variety of conferences and training events—both at Willow Creek's main campus and off-site, across the U.S. and around the world—targeting church leaders in ministry-specific areas such as: evangelism, the arts, children, students, small groups, preaching and teaching, spiritual formation, spiritual gifts, raising up resources, etc.

- **Willow Creek Resources®**—to provide churches with trusted and field-tested ministry resources in such areas as leadership, evangelism, spiritual formation, spiritual gifts, small groups, stewardship, student ministry, children's ministry, the use of the arts—drama, media, contemporary music—and more. For additional information about Willow Creek Resources® call the Customer Service Center at 800-570-9812. Outside the U.S. call 847-765-0070.

- *WillowNet*—the WCA's Internet resource service, which provides access to hundreds of transcripts of Willow Creek messages, drama scripts, songs, videos, and multimedia tools. The system allows users to sort through these elements and download them for a fee. Visit us online at www.willowcreek.com.

- *WCA News*—a quarterly publication to inform you of the latest trends, resources, and information on WCA events from around the world

- *Defining Moments*—a monthly audio journal for church leaders featuring Bill Hybels and other Christian leaders discussing probing issues to help you discover biblical principles and transferable strategies to maximize your church's redemptive potential.

- *The Exchange*—our online classified ads service to assist churches in recruiting key staff for ministry positions.

- **Member Benefits**—includes substantial discounts to WCA training events, a 20 percent discount on all Willow Creek Resources®, access to a Members-Only section on WillowNet, monthly communications, and more. Member Churches also receive special discounts and premier services through WCA's growing number of ministry partners—Select Service Providers.

For specific information about WCA membership, upcoming conferences, and other ministry services contact:

Willow Creek Association
P.O. Box 3188, Barrington, IL 60011-3188
Phone: 847-570-9812
Fax: 847-765-5046
www.willowcreek.com

a place where ...

nobody stands alone!

Small groups, when they're working right, provide a place where you can experience continuous growth and community—the deepest level of community, modeled after the church in Acts 2, where believers are devoted to Christ's teachings and to fellowship with each other.

If you'd like to take the next step in building that kind of small group environment for yourself or for your church, we'd like to help.

The Willow Creek Association in South Barrington, Illinois, hosts an annual Small Groups Conference attended by thousands of church and small group leaders from around the world. Each year we also lead small group training events and workshops in seven additional cities across the country. We offer a number of small group resources for both small groups and small group leaders available to you through your local bookstore and Willow Creek Resources.

If you'd like to learn more, contact the Willow Creek Association at 1-800-570-9812. Or visit us on-line: www.willowcreek.com.

continue the transformation .

PURSUING SPIRITUAL TRANSFORMATION

JOHN ORTBERG, LAURIE PEDERSON, JUDSON POLING

Experience a radical change in how you think and how you live. Forget about trying hard to be a better person. Welcome instead to the richly rewarding process of discovering and growing into the person God made you to be! Developed by Willow Creek Community Church as its core curriculum, this planned, progressive small group approach to spiritual maturity will help you:

- Become more like Jesus
- Recapture the image of God in your life
- Cultivate intimacy with God
- Live your faith everywhere, all the time
- Renew your zest for life

Leader's guide included!

Fully Devoted:
Living Each Day in Jesus' Name   0-310-22073-4

Grace:
An Invitation to a Way of Life   0-310-22074-2

Growth:
Training vs. Trying   0-310-22075-0

Groups:
The Life-Giving Power of Community   0-310-22076-9

Gifts:
The Joy of Serving God   0-310-22077-7

Giving:
Unlocking the Heart of Good Stewardship   0-310-22078-5

Look for Pursuing Spiritual Transformation *at your local bookstore.*

WILLOW
Willow Creek Resources

www.willowcreek.com

ZONDERVAN™

GRAND RAPIDS, MICHIGAN 49530 USA
WWW.ZONDERVAN.COM

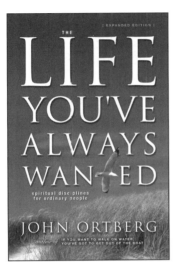

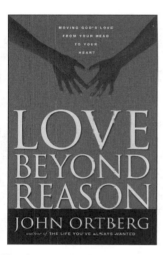

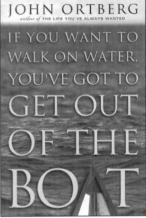

Transform Your Church and Small Groups

Community 101
Gilbert Bilezikian

Written by one of Willow Creek's founders, this resource will help your church become a true community of believers. Bilezikian uses the Bible as his guide to demonstrate the centrality of community in God's plan of salvation and describe how it can be expressed in the daily life of the church.

Softcover – ISBN: 0-310-21741-5

Leading Life-Changing Small Groups
Bill Donahue and the Willow Creek Small Groups Team

Get the comprehensive guidance you need to cultivate life-changing small groups and growing, fruitful believers. Willow Creek's director of adult education and training shares in-depth the practical insights that have made Willow Creek's small group ministry so incredibly effective.

Softcover – ISBN: 0-310-24750-0

Available at your local bookstore!